The Nurses Are Innocent

To Averil, with my
best wishes to you. Steve
was my favorite lunder
radiologist!

Ian

30/04/23

The Nurses Are Innocent

The Digoxin Poisoning Fallacy

Gavin Hamilton, M.D.

DUNDURN
TORONTO

Editor: Allister Thompson
Design: Courtney Horner
Printer: Webcom

Library and Archives Canada Cataloguing in Publication

Hamilton, Gavin
    The nurses are innocent : the digoxin poisoning fallacy / by Gavin Hamilton.

Issued also in electronic formats.
ISBN 978-1-4597-0057-4

    1. Nelles, Susan. 2. Homicide investigation--Ontario--Toronto. 3. Hospital for Sick Children. 4. Ontario. Royal Commission of Inquiry into Certain Deaths at the Hospital for Sick Children and Related Matters. 5. Criminal justice, Administration of--Ontario. 6. Children--Ontario--Toronto--Death. 7. Nurses--Malpractice--Ontario--Toronto. 8. Digoxin--Toxicology. I. Title. II. Title: Digoxin poisoning fallacy.

HV6535.C33T67 2011   363.25'952309713541   C2011-903821-8

1   2   3   4   5   15   14   13   12   11

We acknowledge the support of the **Canada Council for the Arts** and the **Ontario Arts Council** for our publishing program. We also acknowledge the financial support of the **Government of Canada** through the **Canada Book Fund** and **Livres Canada Books**, and the **Government of Ontario** through the **Ontario Book Publishing Tax Credit** and the **Ontario Media Development Corporation**.

Care has been taken to trace the ownership of copyright material used in this book. The author and the publisher welcome any information enabling them to rectify any references or credits in subsequent editions.

J. Kirk Howard, President

Printed and bound in Canada.
www.dundurn.com

Dundurn
3 Church Street, Suite 500
Toronto, Ontario, Canada
M5E 1M2

Gazelle Book Services Limited
White Cross Mills
High Town, Lancaster, England
LA1 4XS

Dundurn
2250 Military Road
Tonawanda, NY
U.S.A. 14150

Contents

In Memoriam

This book is dedicated to Peter Macklem, without whose testimony as an expert witness at the Grange Commission of Inquiry, Susan Nelles might have been tried, convicted, and incarcerated for years as a victim of miscarriage of justice for baby murders — as so many innocent Ontarians have been since that time — based on false interpretations of autopsy findings.

I never met Peter, but he became my friend through our numerous emails and phone calls after his eyes first fell on the manuscript of this book.

He had become one of my heroes through his valiant, almost solitary stand at the Grange Commission of Inquiry. He vigorously denied the validity of digoxin testing of autopsy specimens as measures of digoxin blood levels during life. So convinced was he of the lack of validity of some of the testing being done, that in a lecture to the Canadian Society for Clinical Investigation, he "launched an unbridled attack" on Dr. Cimbura's testing methods at the Centre for Forensic Sciences, so much so that Justice Grange cautioned him to refrain from continuing.

It was because of my reading of the Inquiry that I decided to send him a copy of the manuscript a week before Easter 2010. The following represent verbatim excerpts from the email I got from him a week after he received it:

> April 2, 2010
> Dear Gavin,
> I have thought about little else since I received the manuscript of your book. It must be published!!! A couple of factual and interpretive comments. Grange was pretty helpful to me during my testimony, protecting me from questions like "When did you stop beating your wife?" It wasn't he that demanded an apology, it was the lawyer for Cimbura, I believe, who claimed that lack of controls was damaging to the reputation of his client and I should apologize. I replied that it was not my intention to hurt anyone's reputation and that if I did I was sorry, but nevertheless I was not going to change any testimony on that account. It occurred towards the end of the day, and I had been on the stand since the morning and was getting pretty tired. I immediately regretted my apology and wished I had said something like, "This is a scientific controversy. If one happens to be right and the other person wrong, then one must never apologize for getting closer to the truth. That's the function of science and if someone's reputation suffers as a result, that's also the way science works."

In your book Phyllis Traynor's name is not mentioned. It was my strong impression that when Grange published his report and went on the rubber chicken speaking circuit, he said that he knew murders had been committed and that he knew who had committed them but wasn't allowed to tell, he was implicating Phyllis Traynor, not Susan Nelles. Am I wrong?

You mentioned that you were pressured to drop your investigations but you don't say by whom. Isn't it time to name names and get everything in the open? The time for secrecy is over. When I appeared on the *fifth estate* it was evident that they had a hidden agenda. I believe that they felt that the Ontario Attorney General's Department had put so much time, effort, and publicity into the Nelles case, that it would be politically disastrous if they were proved wrong. I had no interest in entering such a discussion. My involvement was purely scientific, not political. I think I was a big disappointment to the *fifth estate* people.

Anyway, you now have conclusive evidence that there were no murders, so Grange (is he still alive?) should apologize to both Phyllis (what's happened to her?) and to Susan.

I would very much like to meet you, and perhaps we should get together with Graham Stratford in Cobourg or at some other mutually agreeable place. Would you like me to contact Graham and start to organize such a meeting? Also, I have never met Susan Nelles. She came to Montreal once but I was out of town. Do you know her? Could we arrange to meet her somehow, some day?

Thank you so much for sending me your manuscript. Have a happy Easter. Cheers and best,
Peter

Peter and I were both involved in attempting to get the manuscript published. Anne Macklem, Peter's daughter, an editor at UBC Press, suggested Dundurn Press as an excellent publishing house for which the manuscript seemed a good fit.

We had finally set a date to meet for the first time on February 25, 2011, in Cobourg. We both were excited about getting together to discuss the manuscript and become better acquainted.

Tragically, Peter died suddenly at home on February 11, the day before Dundurn Press called to say they were going to proceed with the publication of the book.

Foreword

The cluster of deaths at the Hospital for Sick Children, for which Susan Nelles was charged with murder, was a situation in which diagnostic accuracy was crucial. In order to attribute death to digoxin overdose, as the Grange Commission did, the diagnosis must be accurate. No one on Grange's Ontario Royal Commission of Inquiry, from lawyers, to forensic scientists, and to Grange himself, had expertise in diagnosis, and apart from Dr. D.W. Seccombe, who questioned the accuracy of the radio-immuno-assay used by HSC to measure post mortem digoxin levels, no one with expertise in diagnosis testified before the Grange Commission until I agreed to do so toward the end of the hearings.

I had given a speech to the Canadian Society of Clinical Investigation in which I stated that "all reasonable people will reject the claim of Ontario's Attorney General that exhumed babies were murdered, because the evidence on which it is based is not valid." This brought an immediate invitation to testify before the Commission. I could not be subpoenaed because I was a resident of Quebec.

Here is what I explained to the Commission. Before entering clinical use, one must know the sensitivity and specificity of a diagnostic test. The sensitivity of a test is its ability to detect the disease in the population under study. If the sensitivity is 90 percent, then in a population of 100 subjects in which 10 subjects have the disease, nine will be detected, and one patient will have a false negative result.

The specificity of a test is a measure of how specific the test is for the disease in question. If other diseases or contaminants cause a test to be positive in someone who does not have the disease, this results in a false positive test. If the specificity is also 90 percent, in the same population of 100 subjects in which 10 have the disease and 90 do not, nine healthy subjects will be false positives, incorrectly diagnosed. By combining sensitivity and specificity in our population of 100 subjects in which the disease prevalence is 10 percent of the population, nine out of 10 patients will be correctly diagnosed and one will be missed, but nine patients in the healthy population will be misdiagnosed with the disease, and the diagnosis will be wrong in 10 cases, nine of whom are healthy. There will be 18 positive tests, half of which will be false. Only 50 percent of subjects who tested positive for the disease will actually have it.

Note that the frequency of misdiagnosis depends on the prevalence of the disease within the community. Let's suppose the disease is considerably rarer, with a prevalence of only 1 percent in the community. In a population of 1,000, 10 patients will have the disease, and it will be diagnosed in nine, but now there will be 990 healthy subjects, 10 percent or 99 of whom will have a false positive result. Out of the total number of 108 cases diagnosed with the disease, 99 will be wrong. A false diagnosis will be made in 91 percent of those with positive tests. No information was available to the Grange commission regarding sensitivity, specificity, and predictive accuracy of the post mortem blood tests for digoxin, and it was not until I testified that these methods of assessing diagnostic tests were mentioned. To my knowledge, the sensitivity, specificity, and diagnostic accuracy of post mortem testing for digoxin remains unknown to this day.

Even worse, no one knew what the "normal" values of post mortem blood digoxin are, and probably still don't.

Pathological diagnosis is classically made by detecting structural abnormalities in body tissues, which are characteristic for specific diseases. For most conditions the abnormal structure, which permits accurate pathological diagnosis, persists after death. Unfortunately, there is no characteristic structural abnormality of digoxin overdose. For this reason forensic investigators had to rely on biochemical abnormalities rather than structural ones. But with death there are profound changes in the body's chemistry.

The vital chemical processes that keep us alive, such as using the sources of energy supplied by oxygen and food and eliminating waste products through the lungs, skin, and urinary and gastrointestinal tracts, cease. The pumps that keep the chemistry inside the cells entirely different from the outside stop functioning.

As described in detail by Gavin Hamilton, this is particularly important with regard to digoxin, which binds to the heart and skeletal muscle. If death releases this binding so that digoxin returns to the blood, the "normal" therapeutic values of blood digoxin would be quite different after death than during life. The Grange Commission failed to examine this possibility. Unfortunately, in my testimony before the Grange Commission, I only made the point that so-called "normal" digoxin levels were unknown in the exhumed babies. As Dr. Hamilton points out, the same arguments can be made for post mortem digoxin levels, and I wish I had been smart enough to make this argument.

The post mortem diagnosis of digoxin poisoning used by the forensic scientists in both freshly dead and exhumed babies, i.e. every single baby who was thought to have been murdered, was based upon a single biochemical test without knowledge of the normal values. In my view this constitutes medical malpractice, resulting from the lack of a single person on the Commission who had any knowledge of medical diagnosis and its pitfalls. This type of highly flawed evidence cannot be used to determine that murder was committed.

Dr. Gavin Hamilton must be applauded for having the courage to print the truth about the deaths of babies at Toronto's Hospital for Sick Children and the terrible ordeal that Susan Nelles unjustly suffered as a result. His extensive research showing that a toxin found in natural rubber, mercaptobenzothiazole, which is chemically a digoxin-like substance, might well have been the culprit in the babies' deaths, is compelling. He clearly demonstrates that explanations other than serial murders account for the cluster of infant deaths at HSC.

What can be learned from this black stain on Canada's judicial system? One lesson certainly stands out: we cannot ever again allow a group of unqualified amateur diagnosticians to make life and death decisions about such important matters as potential serial murders.

Royal Commissions must have expertise in the problem at hand beyond those of members of the legal profession. In the Susan Nelles case, an expert in clinical pharmacology should have been a permanent member of the Commission. In similar cases, every effort to avoid a miscarriage of justice must be made by including individuals with appropriate expertise. This will maximize the chance of arriving at the truth. Sadly, the Grange Commission failed to do so.

Peter Macklem

Preface

This small book really represents a part of my memoirs and is composed of two parallel stories. The first evolved out of a radiological technique I developed showing the blood supply to the kidneys on a routine X-ray examination of the urinary tract after an intravenous injection of a radio-opaque dye (an IVP). This resulted in my performing at least 1,000 of these examinations every year, but these injections were not without risk of occasional severe reactions and, rarely, deaths. No deaths occurred in my series.

It describes the discovery of an insidious unsuspected allergenic and toxic chemical that contaminated injected X-ray dyes, drugs, IV fluids, and blood transfusions from the rubber parts of disposable plastic syringes and intravenous apparatus. Contamination of the X-ray dye by this chemical was proven to be associated with two series of allergic reactions in my small private radiology office over a four-year period, with one life-threatening anaphylactic shock occurring in each series.

The second story examines a mysterious epidemic in 1980–1981 of baby deaths in the cardiac wards of the Hospital for Sick Children (HSC) in Toronto, Ontario. A total of 24 deaths were attributed to poisoning from intentional over-dosage with the heart drug digoxin, and blame was attributed to a nurse.

The HSC story showed timing of the major events coexisting with major parts of the first story. Some of those people involved in each of these storylines were aware of a number of details of the other story, but had no idea of the intimate interconnections.

A suggestion that made it possible to connect the two tales came from Dr. Ed Napke of Nepean, Ontario, a physician who spent his life involved in Canada's adverse drug reaction reporting while the head of Canada's Product Related Disease Division, Health Protection Branch, at the Department of National Health in Ottawa. Dr. Napke wondered if the cause of the reactions to X-ray dyes that I had uncovered could be related to the HSC baby deaths. This suggestion paved the way to connecting one end of these parallel chains of events.

On another stage on another continent, at this same time, another intimately connected drama was playing out — a relatively unheralded epidemic of poisoning was being uncovered, involving 91 babies, again on a single hospital ward. It was only by chance in 1992 that the author uncovered this baby poisoning episode, quite late in this story.

Developments unfolding over the last two years linked the chains at the other end, forming a circle around the Toronto baby death murder theory. A recognizable pattern emerged, materializing out of the shadows of the stage on which the mass murder theory had been enacted.

Introduction

It was truly a blessing to have taken my pre-university schooling in St. Thomas, a small city in southwestern Ontario, where the streets were so safe that the outside screen doors could be left unlocked day and night in the summer. The public and elementary school teachers had been carefully selected and were of a quality that one would expect in the best private schools, giving St. Thomas students an academic advantage over many other areas when the standardized compulsory grade thirteen graduation examinations had to be taken. It was on the basis of these Ontario Department of Education examinations that one could attend universities and on which university scholarships were awarded.

I entered University of Western Ontario (UWO) in 1949, with the UWO Board of Governor's prize in Physics and Chemistry and a Board of Governors scholarship in six subjects (sciences, mathematics, and English). Although enrolling in honours physics, at the end of first year I felt a need to change direction, being drawn towards a career in medicine. Fortunately, I was allowed to transfer to the second year of pre meds, going on to graduate with an MD in 1955.

In 1955, I entered into a five-year internal medicine residency program at Victoria Hospital, London, under Dr. F.S. Brien, the UWO Professor of Medicine. At the end of this training period, one would be qualified to write the Royal College of Physicians of Canada examinations for a specialist degree in internal medicine.

Dr. Brien's fascination with therapeutics, and his keen interest in the spectrum of adverse reactions to the various pharmaceuticals being prescribed, led to his appointment as the supervisor of the Ontario Medical Association's Adverse Drug Reaction Reporting Program. Dr. Brien's intense interest in adverse drug effects and their reporting to a central agency became indelibly imprinted on my own subsequent behaviour.

In 1957, at the end of two years of the internal medicine residency, my life circumstances directed me out of the internal medicine program and into the world in a career in family medicine (general practice, as it was called then) in London, Ontario. I found myself launched into practice on a wave of Asiatic influenza that was surging across the world. I was almost inundated by the caseload as I dealt with many house calls and follow-up office calls on these patients, many of which had no family doctor. Immediately, I established a relatively busy practice, a feat that otherwise would have taken at least a few years in the city of London in that era.

I had always been interested in therapeutics, but, like Dr. Brien, I was determined to use as few medications as possible, to reduce the chance of adverse drug reactions and interactions, and to keep costs down for my patients who were mostly trying to make ends meet. I had been taught to weigh carefully the risks associated with medical or surgical treatment against the risks of the medical problem being treated. He cautioned to be aware of the adverse reactions a pharmaceutical might cause and adverse interactions with other drugs that were being taken concurrently.

This philosophy led me to make a practice of setting some time aside on Wednesday mornings to listen to the pharmaceutical company representatives as they gave their "spiel" on pharmaceutical products, some new, some old. I listened, questioned, and learned from the exercise. It was during one of these drug "rep" sessions, in 1959 or 1960, that a new anti-nausea drug was being promoted for the nausea of "morning sickness" during pregnancy. That drug was thalidomide. It was touted as being greatly superior to Gravol (dimenhydrenate), the drug I recommended, if any, for my pregnant patients. The rep explained that they had used new computerized methods to analyze the results on this drug. He boasted that by using a sample group of pregnant patients and by using new computerized analyses, they got results in six months that would normally take two years.

At this point, I interrupted his presentation by stating that I refused to use thalidomide because a pregnancy takes ten lunar months, and even that length of time would be insufficient to prove it was safe. That was just a casual remark on his part, but was a stroke of immense good luck for me and especially for my pregnant patients. I was delivering 75 babies per year then, and, as I learned later, thalidomide could have had devastating effects on the developing limbs in some of the babies I was delivering. Thalidomide became the most vigorously promoted drug of any that I had encountered up to that time. The many free samples that were mailed to me almost weekly were disposed of. The mailing of pharmaceutical samples was made illegal a few years later.

Family medicine filled me with excitement and a feeling of fulfillment, treating patients in my office, making house calls and hospital calls, and delivering babies. As far as their health needs were concerned, I treated my patients as a shepherd tends his flock, trying to deal with them equally.

However, at the end of nine years, I was forced to examine the pressures of my daily life. A significant elevation in my blood pressure reflected the effects of the stress from sleep deprivation, from the phone calls almost every night (in the middle of the night), the many house calls, the afternoon, evening, and Saturday morning office hours, and the delivery of babies, which often occurred in the middle of the night, interrupting my sleep.

It was at this time in late 1965, after nine years of a busy family medicine practice, that Dr. Dick Treleaven, a radiologist friend who had started his own medical career as a family practitioner, suggested a career in diagnostic radiology. Until that time the thought of a specialty in diagnostic radiology hadn't entered my mind. After my exposure to family medicine and the enjoyment I derived from delivering babies and looking after the mothers and children, if another specialty were to be pursued, it more likely would have been obstetrics and gynecology. Nonetheless, the advantages of a more regulated life and considering my interest in physics, the specialty of diagnostic radiology occupied my thoughts.

As a result of these serious and potentially life-changing deliberations, I submitted an application for a residency in diagnostic radiology, under Professor G. G. Copestake at Victoria Hospital, London. I was accepted into the program and started as a diagnostic radiology resident on July 1, 1966. Almost instantly, I became totally immersed in and fascinated by diagnostic radiology, delighting in the opportunity to integrate divergent pieces of information — the X-ray results, together with the patient's history, physical examination, and laboratory tests — leading to a definite diagnosis or, at least, a manageable small list of disease possibilities. All the most interesting and diagnostically perplexing patients passed through the doors of the Department of Radiology. It was a place for medical armchair detection at its best. To help make ends meet for my young family, I worked one night a week as the emergency physician in the emergency department of Victoria Hospital.

With my previous two years of internal medicine residency, only three years were necessary to complete the requirements for taking the Diagnostic Radiology Fellowship examinations. The three years required to complete the radiology residency program flew by quickly, but it was in an atmosphere of subdued intensity. The intensity factor increased dramatically as the spectre of the September 1969 specialist written exams approached. Without a diploma as a certified specialist, or as a Fellowship specialist, one could not practice as a diagnostic radiologist. The Fellowship diploma examinations at that time required an intimate knowledge of internal medicine, so half of my study hours were spent buried in such texts.

When the written examinations began in September 1969, there was a room full of specialist hopefuls gathered in rows of school desks, cramped together in a hot, stuffy, non air-conditioned classroom, with several serious, stern-looking monitors patrolling the aisles. It was very regimented, reminiscent of the standardized Ontario Department of Education high school final examinations (all students in Ontario were required to write them to qualify for university and for scholarships). The tension was extreme, but there was a lot at stake. All had been through at least four extra years of strenuous postgraduate resident training, subsisting on an annual salary of three thousand dollars, hoping to obtain a specialist diploma.

I wrote the examinations for certification and those for the Canadian Royal College Fellowship in Diagnostic Radiology — five long, nail-biting examinations in two and a half days. Then, there were the weeks of waiting — studying for the oral examinations that you would have to face, only if you had passed the written examinations.

Finally, there was a knock on my door, and the postman hand-delivered the registered letter from Ottawa that required a signature from the addressee. I can imagine only a few candidates who would open their letter confidently knowing that they had passed. It had been fourteen years since I last wrote an examination, and, I must admit, my hands shook as I ripped open the letter — as a man is wont to do under such circumstances. To the extreme relief of all in my family, words "successfully passed" leaped off the page. I was successful in both the Certification and the Fellowship examinations. Feelings of joy, relief, and thanks spread through our household that day.

With the written examinations successfully over, the celebrating was quickly displaced by focusing on preparing for the last act of this play. The Fellowship orals never were performed as comedy, but often wore the mask of tragedy — with failure — and having to come back next year and try again. In preparation for these orals, during the daylight hours, I concentrated on studying internal medicine, the basic sciences, radiological physics, and diagnostic radiology writings.

In relative silence, when the Department of Radiology corridors were empty, I spent many late evenings at Victoria Hospital going through filing cabinets full of the teaching file X-rays. I put aside those film envelopes in which I couldn't immediately spot the abnormality, and later studied these again, but much more intently. As I repeatedly worked my way through the files, gradually the pile of "missed" diagnoses got smaller and smaller, until a climactic point was reached when there was no pile at all. I was as ready as I would ever be for the film reading components of the examination, but that readiness could not be equated to complacency. There were so many obscure abnormalities buried in the X-ray films in the teaching files of other radiology departments — X-rays that I had never seen — perhaps with abnormalities of a type that I had never seen.

The book work, added to the experience gained from the internal medicine and radiology residency positions and, unquestionably, the practical experience of nine years of family medicine, helped me considerably that November when I was grilled by a group from different specialist fields during three sets of the Fellowship oral examinations at the Toronto General Hospital. The panel of "judges" confronting me seemed like Spanish Inquisitors of another continent and another century, and my fate was in their hands.

In an oral examination setting, one's senses are turned on full, amplified by the instinctive feral fight-or-flight reaction of our fear-induced adrenaline output. Having completed two oral sessions, it came down to the final question-and-answer film reading session. In this last oral, after about twenty minutes of questions from a hematologist, an orthopedic surgeon, and a radiologist, it was the radiologist who was to be my last Inquisitor.

He held in his hand ten envelopes, each with an X-ray film in which there would be a significant but subtle abnormality to be detected (or missed). The method of self-examination I had used during my teaching file late evening sessions was about to be subjected to the ultimate test.

I was able to detect the abnormality soon after the X-ray was placed on the view box with the first nine of his ten cases. With the final film, he seemed to take a little more time extracting it from the envelope, as if it was his favourite, the most subtle of his teaching file films — a potential *coup de grâce* was about to be administered.

However, he seemed to be somewhat taken aback when, just as he took his hand away from placing this film on the view box, I said: "This film shows faint patchy sclerosis and demineralization of both femoral heads, suggesting avascular necrosis of the femoral heads [faint changes in the bone density of the heads of the hip bones that suggested loss of blood supply to these areas]."

He started to ask me another question about the film, but in the middle of his sentence he took it from the view box, put it in the envelope, said that that was all, and escorted me out of the room with his hand on my shoulder. I knew I had passed the ten "quickie" cases that ended my ordeal — but there had been many questions posed, and many answers given in the earlier part of this oral, and in the other two oral sessions.

The required years of training and the written and oral examinations were done, and now the period of waiting for the result of all the efforts was compressed into a palpably intense few hours of pins and needles until the results would be revealed, one candidate's name at a time.

A few hours later (which felt more like years), I was sweating it out, sitting in a small, hot, stuffy, dark, and dismal conference room in the basement of the TGH with all the other Fellowship candidates for several different specialties — all anxious, speechless, and utterly attentive to the point of fixation. As the names were being read — painfully slowly — of those who had successfully passed the orals, I virtually catapulted out of my seat when I heard mine, and floated up to the podium to receive the Fellowship diploma, formally inscribed in old English script and Latin.

I was now allowed to use the coveted specialist designation, FRCP(C) (Fellow of the Royal College of Physicians and Surgeons of Canada) after my name. With a big sigh of relief, I realized the ordeal was finally over. Elatedly and hurriedly, I sought out the nearest pay phone to tell my wife and young children the exciting news.

PART I

Toxic and Allergenic Medical Rubber Contaminants in Injections

One

A Simple New Technique to Show Kidney Vascularity

In January 1970 I started my career as a full-fledged diagnostic radiologist at Westminster Hospital in London, Ontario. At the time, it was operated by the Canadian Department of Veteran's Affairs and was dedicated to caring for the hospital needs of our active armed forces and the veterans of two world wars. The X-ray equipment was rudimentary by teaching hospital standards, without image intensified fluoroscopy equipment and with inadequate facilities for performing arteriography. However, when confronted with limited facilities, one is challenged to incorporate ingenuity in circumventing the deficiencies encountered while performing one's duties.

Among the many procedures a radiologist is called upon to perform is to obtain radiographs (X-ray pictures) of the excretion of a radio-opaque dye that is injected into an arm vein with the dye being actively eliminated by the kidney tubules. The dye, being opaque to X-rays, outlines the excretory portions of the kidneys as well as the ureters and bladder. Since it involves the ability to excrete the dye from the circulating blood, it yields evidence of renal physiology and pathophysiology as well as the anatomy of the urinary collecting system. This X-ray examination is called an intravenous (or excretory) pyelogram, or IVP.

The dye traces the path of William Harvey's circulation of the blood.[1] Injected into an arm vein, it mixes with the arm's venous blood, which drains into the superior vena cava that enters the right side of the heart. The right heart pumps the dye-containing venous blood through the lungs into the left heart and thence into the aorta, the body's main artery. The aorta delivers this arterial blood, containing the dye, to all parts of the body. The kidneys, with their very rich capillary circulation, receive 25 per cent of the blood pumped from the heart. Very quickly, the kidneys remove unwanted breakdown products of metabolism, also clearing the radio-opaque dyes from the circulating blood, outlining on X-ray, the excretory portions of the urinary system — the intra-renal collecting parts (the calyces and pelves), the ureters, and the urinary bladder.

A few seconds after slowly injecting dye intravenously for one of these procedures, a patient commented that he had experienced a peculiar warm sensation, or taste, in the back of his tongue and throat, shortly after the end of the injection of the dye into an arm vein. Because of this comment, I started injecting the dye more rapidly, discovering (as I had hoped) that with a more rapid injection, almost all patients experienced this warmth. This sensation of warmth became much more pronounced than with a slow injection. Furthermore, almost all patients experienced a similar fairly pronounced warm sensation in the anogenital regions, a few seconds after the oral sensation.

The warm taste announced that the dye injected into an arm vein had reached the arterial and capillary circulations of the mouth; a few seconds later, the warm anogenital sensation indicated that it had passed through the abdominal aorta to reach the arterial and capillary systems in the anogenital area. This was a "Eureka!" moment, because I sensed that this observation could have significant practical applications.

In my two years as an internal medicine resident, it was known that patients with a failing heart had a slow circulation time. Therefore, if one could measure the time it would take for venous blood in the arm to enter the superior vena cava, go through the right side of the heart, through the lungs, and then into the aorta and into the arteries of the body, it would be a measure of the circulation time. In the 1950s, a technique was devised to inject a solution that contained a bitter-tasting bile salt (decholin sodium) into an arm vein, then measuring the number of seconds it would take to enter the arterial system of the tongue, where a bitter taste would be experienced. The number of seconds between the injection into an arm vein and the bitter taste was called the circulation time. A prolonged circulation time would indicate a failing heart. What wasn't appreciated at that time was that the two cubic centimeters of injected fluid containing the bile salt would often linger too long in the veins of the axilla, which were often kinked when the arm was at the patient's side, leading to many prolonged circulation time measurements in patients not in heart failure. Specific timing of its arrival in the abdominal aorta after such an injection was thus impossible.

However, when a larger volume of fluid was injected (60 mL, 2 ounces of X-ray dye), and if the patient's arm was abducted and elevated, I wondered if there would be a more constant time interval after a rapid injection, when the hot oral sensation occurred as the dye arrived through the aorta and into the arterial system of the tongue. It would then be a matter of the time interval between the patient getting the hot taste and the time of maximum demonstration in the rich capillary beds of the kidneys. If so, on a simple intravenous examination (an IVP), one could show the blood supply to the kidneys as a bonus, something that could be done only rather crudely at that time by radio isotope scans, or more clearly by much more invasive arteriographic techniques.

Accurate timing of the arrival of the dye in the kidney following the rapid intravenous dye injection would result in quite a significant concentration of the radio-opaque dye in the rich capillary circulation in the kidneys. This could potentially make the kidney tissue stand out much more clearly on an X-ray taken at this specific time than at any other time, when one was looking at the excreted dye in the collecting system of the kidneys, in the ureters, and in the bladder. All the X-ray findings of a normally performed IVP examination would still be obtained. Since the kidneys receive 25 percent of the body's arterial flow, the slow flow through the rich capillary blood supply in the kidney tissue might yield a pronounced X-ray image of what one could call the capillary nephrogram, or the vascular nephrogram.[2]

After I varied the timing of this "capillary nephrogram" film in a few dozen rapidly injected IVPs, I determined that the radio-opaque dye injection indeed did outline this rich capillary bed of the kidneys, defining the size of the kidneys and allowing them to be compared in their size and relative vascularity. In addition it was not uncommon to have the aorta and renal arteries outlined by the dye, something that was unheard of in a normal IVP X-ray study. The best time interval for showing the renal vascularity was six to 10 seconds after the patient felt the warm throat sensation. Ninety-five percent of patients experienced this oral sensation with a rapid injection of the dye. Those that didn't taste the dye had the capillary nephrogram taken when they developed facial flushing, or experienced the anogenital warmth.

I designed a foot pump, using a simple lever system, an inverted 50 mL disposable plastic syringe, and a 16-gauge butterfly needle to deliver 50 mL of warmed radio-opaque dye into an arm vein in as little as three seconds (Figures 1 and 2), further enhancing the capillary nephrogram.[3]

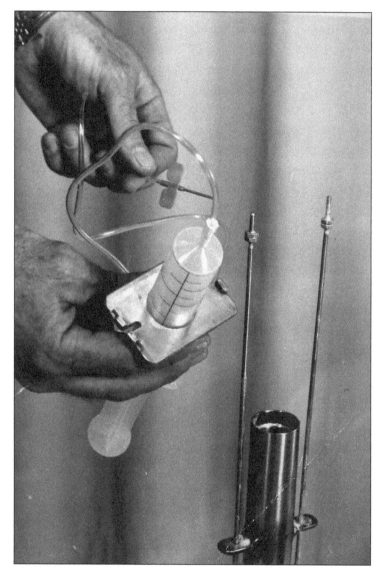

Figure 1

The capillary nephrogram in this technique for an IVP now could reveal a smaller, less vascular kidney on one side, the hallmark of a narrowing (stenosis) of a kidney artery, a correctable cause of severe high blood pressure. Also, on a simple IVP, one could often differentiate between a spherical kidney mass, which had no blood supply (a simple cyst), and a vascular mass, which usually represented a malignant tumor.

It was the amount of physiological and pathological information gleaned by this new technique, using a single additional film (the capillary nephrogram film) that was destined to have me, in my lifetime, probably injecting more patients with X-ray dyes for IVPs than any single radiologist in Ontario, if not in the entire world, thereby providing me with a large body of experience in the effects of these dyes on patients.

Between 1971 and 1973, this method of timing, while using 100 mL (instead of the usual 50 mL) of rapidly injected dye intravenously through a 16-gauge butterfly needle, allowed the abdominal aorta to be outlined (a radiological procedure known as intravenous aortography) in 150 patients at Westminster DVA Hospital in London. Until this time, many serial radiographs (X-ray pictures) of the abdomen, at one- to two-second intervals, were required after the intravenous dye injection to show the aorta as it was well-outlined fleetingly with the radio-opaque dye on one or two of the films.

By timing the first of five radiographs to coincide with the patient signifying when the hot taste was first noticed, only five radiographs were needed, one every two seconds.

The use of a simple technique known as film subtraction aortography further enhanced the image of the aorta.

To demonstrate how this technique works, I pasted 99 small, similar silver stars on an 8 by 11 sheet of paper and took a photograph of the page with a medium-format camera mounted on a tripod. Without changing the position of the camera or the paper, I added one more similar star to

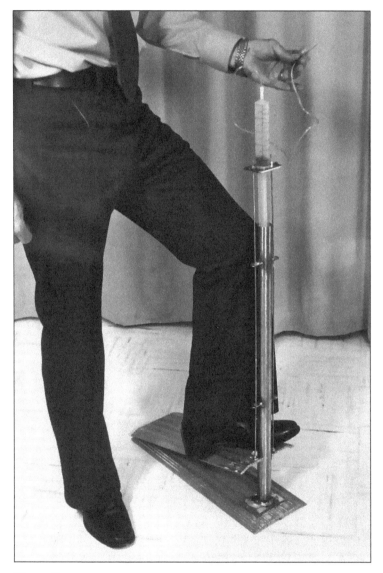

Figure 2

Figure 3
A photograph of the negative copy of a negative of 100 stars superimposed on the negative of these same stars, with one star added.

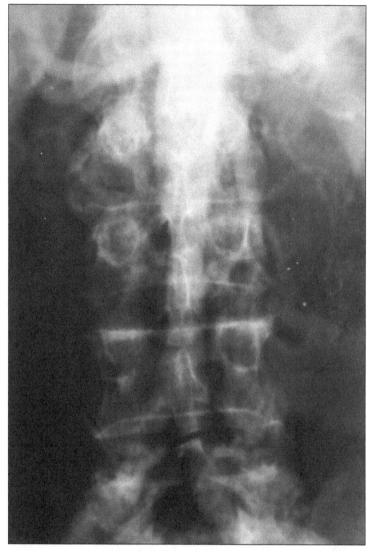

Figure 4
An intravenous aortogram, showing the abdominal aorta and the
renal, mesenteric, and common iliac arteries, following the rapid
intravenous injection of 100 ml of a radio-opaque contrast agent
(sodium iothalamate), with this film being taken immediately
after the patient experienced a hot taste in the oropharynx,
signifying the arrival of the contrast bolus in the arterial system.

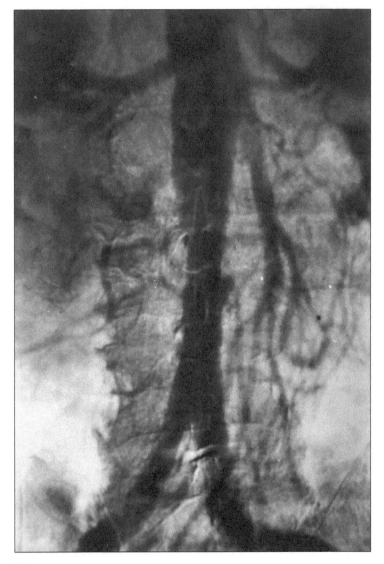

Figure 5

the page. No one could casually appreciate where the star had been added.

I then took another photograph of this page with the 100 stars. I made a positive transparency of this image. When the positive image of the page containing the added star is superimposed on the negative of the original with 99 stars, the added star leaps out of the page, with the 99 stars showing only faintly (See Figure 3). This is a photographic subtraction technique.

The X-ray film subtraction technique was accomplished by taking an X-ray film of the same area immediately before the injection (the control film), then making a negative of this X-ray. When this negative was superimposed on a positive X-ray film showing the dye in the aorta, the background images, such as the bones, faded out and the new image information (the X-ray dye) stood out (See photographs of an abdominal aortogram without and with the film subtraction technique — Figures 4 and 5). A similar technique, using digital fluoroscopic imaging equipment, became popular a few years later (digital subtraction angiography), in X-ray departments with much more modern X-ray equipment.

This intravenous aortography technique was superior to methods in use at the time and could have replaced the previously used method, and many of the more invasive trans lumbar aortography examinations. However, intravenous aortography and most of the trans lumbar aortograms were superseded by the introduction of the Seldinger method of threading a catheter into the aorta from the femoral artery in the groin and injecting the X-ray dyes directly into the aorta, or injecting dye selectively into specific arteries, such as in coronary arteriography (selective catheter arteriography).

In 1973, I left Westminster Hospital to open a small private office with modern diagnostic X-ray private office equipment, in an office building where, simultaneously, two urology professors also chose to relocate their private offices.

From 1973 until to 1994, the rapid injection IVP technique was continued in this private office setting, injecting the dye manually in about six to 10 seconds in as many as eight patients per day on occasion.[4] The kidney vascular phase was now routinely imaged even more distinctly by taking a single thick X-ray slice (a tomogram, or "zonogram") through the kidneys, eight to 10 seconds after the patients tasted the dye. Because there were two urologists in the office building and because other clinicians recognized the value of this technique, approximately 1,000 IVPs were performed annually in this private office setting, more than in most hospitals, and almost all were injected by one radiologist.

My publication of articles in journals, and my teaching of diagnostic radiology technologists and residents in the Family Medicine Certification program, was recognized by my appointment as a UWO Assistant Professor of Radiology, a distinction I held from 1973 to 2000.

Two

Physiologic and Allergic Reactions to IVP Dye Injections

There have always been patients who exhibited various types of allergic reactions to radio-opaque dyes that contain iodine in their molecular structure. Even in the 1970s, diagnostic radiologists across the world used these dyes extensively for IVPs, arteriography, venography, and heart chamber studies. The reactions varied in severity, ranging from flushing, itching, and hives (urticaria), to the more serious reactions of asthma, and life-threatening anaphylactic shock and edema of the larynx, that might require a tracheotomy to save the patient's life. The incidence of the severe, life-threatening reactions to IVP dye injections was about one per 1,000 injections, with deaths from X-ray dye injections being quite infrequent (about one per 100,000 cases).[1]

In my lifetime series of well over 15,000 IVPs, one to a few hives occurred frequently — in about 5 percent of patients. This was more common than in most series of IVPs, but all patients were questioned carefully to determine if they had any itchy areas, and these areas were examined for hives. Almost all complaining of itching had one or more hives, often in areas under the routinely worn hospital gowns (where they weren't overtly apparent, and in other X-ray facilities where they might not have been examined).

Those involved in the OMA's Adverse Drug Reporting Program must have noticed that they were receiving more reports of minor reactions from X-ray dye injections from a single small private radiology office in London, Ontario, than they were receiving from diagnostic centres using far more X-ray dyes, because hives were found where others wouldn't have looked, and because all reactions were being reported fastidiously.

In 1966, during my first year as a radiology resident, when it was routine to use 2-ounce (60 mL) all-glass syringes for the injection of IVP X-ray dyes, infrequently these syringes broke in the hands of the residents who did the injecting, sometimes inflicting hand lacerations that required suturing in the emergency department. Later in my residency years, unbreakable disposable plastic syringes, with natural rubber seals on the syringe plunger tips, replaced the glass syringes, a practice that was being adopted almost universally at that time. The residents welcomed this change, because the risk of lacerations from the breaking of glass syringes was now eliminated.

Dr. G.G. Copestake, the Professor of Radiology and the Director of Victoria Hospital's Department of Radiology, was an astute observer. He warned the residents that there would be times when clusters of reactions would occur with certain manufacturers' lots of dyes. When this pattern was suspected, Dr. Copestake would send the lots of dye back to the manufacturer, asking for tests to be done to see if any cause for reactions could be ascertained. He commented that nothing unusual was ever reported to him, but the clusters of reactions would seem to vanish suddenly when a new batch of dye was introduced.

When I started in my position as a radiologist at Westminster Hospital — and throughout my career — I kept careful records of all IVP injections. The documentation included a history of previous allergic reactions, the age, sex, skin and eye colour, the number of seconds after the injection of the appearance of the warmth in the throat and anogenital regions, and the degree of this warmth and history of previous X-ray dye injections. Reactions to the injection, such as facial flushing, nausea, and vomiting, and any allergic reactions were recorded. The oral warmth and the anogenital warmth sensations, as well as the facial flushing, were considered to be normal (physiological) responses and were not classified as allergic in origin, each occurring in 95 percent of cases. Careful notes were made, not only of the nature of any IVP reactions occurring, but the patient's response to the treatment instituted.

Those with a history of asthma were referred to hospitals for their IVPs. After two anaphylactic reactions in two months in patients taking beta adrenergic blocking agents, patients taking these drugs were also referred to hospitals if IVPs were demanded, because I was concerned that this group of drugs was predisposed to anaphylaxis.[2]

I always kept my finger on the patient's pulse at the wrist before the injection, with the patient's arm abducted and elevated during the injection, so that all the dye, which was heavier than blood, would flow out of the arm veins, into the larger veins, and thence into the superior vena cava, the largest upper-body vein. My finger was returned to the patient's pulse at the wrist at the end of the injection phase and was kept there until three minutes after the injection, to detect any change in the patient's pulse rate, and to detect any drop in pulse pressure. A drop in blood pressure and elevation of the pulse rate could signal the onset of anaphylactic shock from a severe allergic reaction to the injection, a dreaded complication of X-ray dye injections and one that can be fatal, even when treated appropriately.

A trolley, on which was an emergency tray, was at the patient's side until the patient left the room after the completion of the IVP. This tray held only essential emergency drugs and medical devices — ampoules of adrenaline (1:1,000 aqueous solution, unquestionably the most important single drug to be used in significant allergic reactions), intravenous cortisone ampoules (Solu-Cortef, Pfizer, 100 mg, in the early cases, increased to as much as 1,000 mg in later years), needles, syringes, and an ampoule of intravenous glucose (in case a diabetic suffered an episode of a serious insulin-induced drop in blood glucose). No antihistamine ampoules were allowed on the tray. (I can still remember Dr. Brien, the Professor of Medicine, saying that no life had ever been saved by antihistamines, and that administering them would waste valuable time when a serious reaction was being treated.) The intravenous cortisone's purpose was not to stop the allergic response, because the cascade of events had already occurred; it was to help the patient to survive the state of shock when a profound drop in blood pressure prevailed.

If a significant drop in blood pressure developed, the head of the table was tilted down to increase blood flow to the brain and to make the venous blood in the legs enter the circulation (like a mini transfusion). The pulse at the wrist becoming faint or imperceptible signalled a marked drop in blood pressure. When that happened, no attempt was made to measure the blood pressure; it was vital to direct all efforts to saving the patient's life, rather than trying (usually futilely) to get blood pressure readings while working around the X-ray equipment surrounding the patient.[3] Oxygen would be administered if there was even a suggestion of shortness of breath.

When there were only a few hives, empirically, the patients were treated with two glasses of cold water, and were told to drink extra water when they went home to flush out the dye more quickly from their systems. Patients were assured thus that something was being done for their hives — and a reasonable explanation was being offered for the method of treatment. Those with more than three hives were treated routinely and empirically with 0.5 mL of 1:1,000 aqueous adrenalin, injected subcutaneously. In the cases requiring adrenaline, the redness and itching subsided in a few minutes and the hives were usually gone within 30 minutes.

This empirical criterion proved its worth when a 13-year-old girl developed more than three hives and had adrenaline injected two minutes before she developed hoarseness and slight difficulty in breathing. This indicated the onset of laryngeal edema, a dreaded complication of an allergic reaction that commonly would require an emergency tracheotomy. I spoke gently and calmly to her, cautioning her to breathe as easily as she could so as not to further irritate her larynx, and I administered a dose of intravenous cortisone (Solu-Cortef, 100 mg). I continued to talk softly, acting as if this was an everyday occurrence, while keeping my finger on her pulse (not telling her that a scalpel was near at hand, in case I had to do my first tracheotomy). Her voice stabilized in this hoarse state and remained so as she was taken by ambulance to the emergency department of a hospital close by, where her voice gradually returned to normal.

In two patients who had received this treatment I thought might be about to die (because of the onset of a sighing type of respiration), a small intravenous dose of the aqueous adrenaline was administered. Although this did not result in a palpable pulse, the sighing respiration vanished and the patients brightened up. Both survived in good health after a short hospital stay. One of these patients was a nurse who was aware of the significance of this sequence of events; he returned to my office two days later, offering thanks for the potentially life-saving treatment administered by our staff.

The X-ray dye was always injected through a "butterfly" needle that remained taped in place in an arm vein, until the examination was finished. These butterfly needles were connected to a length of polyethylene tubing and to the 50 mL disposable plastic syringes used to inject the dye. These syringes, still connected to the needles' tubing, were also taped to the patient's arm. The butterfly needles, already in a vein, proved to be a valuable lifeline in treating patients who developed life-threatening reactions — and they would still be in place on their arrival at a hospital emergency department. Otherwise, in such an emergency in a patient with no measurable blood pressure, finding a vein into which to establish an IV lifeline could be very difficult.

The 50 mL dye ampoules and the 50 mL disposable plastic syringes used for the dye injections were always bought in large lots, and the manufacturers' lot numbers were recorded.

Three

Anaphylactic Shock Following an IVP Dye Injection

Over a period of several weeks in the early spring of 1983, a clustering of increased minor side effects was suspected following IVP dye injections. These fairly mild but nevertheless disquieting reactions included an increase in, and a prolongation of, the normally occurring facial flushing (this increased flushing sometimes extended to include more of the body), an increase in the incidence and number of hives, and an increased incidence of nausea and vomiting. The flushing and the hives disappeared shortly after the administration of adrenaline subcutaneously (if adrenaline was deemed necessary). Switching to another manufacturer's dye lot did not seem to alter the incidence of these reactions.

Then, disaster struck! One patient developed a profound drop in blood pressure, with the pulse at the wrist, which had been strong, becoming faint to imperceptible as the dreaded complication of anaphylactic shock set in.

Immediately, emergency treatment was instituted. A subcutaneous injection of adrenaline (0.5 mg of 1:10,000 aqueous adrenaline) and cortisone (100 mg of Solu-Cortef) intravenously were administered in quick succession. Oxygen was given by mask and the head of the X-ray table was lowered to increase the blood supply to the brain. The emergency tray, being immediately at hand, allowed the start of treatment within seconds of the drop in the patient's pulse pressure.

An ambulance was called as the adrenaline was being injected, and the patient was in the hospital emergency department 30 minutes after the anaphylactic shock started. Although the hospital emergency staff had some initial difficulty stabilizing the patient's blood pressure, the patient survived without after effects and was discharged on the following day.

In such cases the radiology technologists and myself worked as a team with quiet efficiency, as if it were an everyday occurrence. A careful observer would have noticed our dilated pupils, cold hands, and just a trace of a tremor from our own adrenaline responses.

Four

A Hidden and Unsuspected Allergenic Hazard in Pharmaceutical Rubber

Improbable coincidences have often occurred in my life. One such coincidence was that, at precisely this time, I happened to read a short article in the *Medical Post* describing the discovery of particulate contaminants in the fluid contents of B-D Plastipak syringes, the brand of syringes I was using at the time of the anaphylactic shock reaction. These particles had originated from the internal surfaces of the disposable syringes. Immediately, I wondered if the dye injected was being contaminated by an allergenic substance associated with the disposable plastic syringes — and not from the dye. To that time, I had focused only on allergic reactions related to the dye itself. Allergies associated with contamination from the disposable syringes could explain why my recent series of reactions continued after changing to a new lot of dye.

Having no idea where to go from there, I phoned the Ontario Medical Association's Adverse Drug Reporting Program, asking where I could send my syringes to be tested for contaminants. I was directed to the Bureau of Medical Devices in Ottawa (BMD), a branch of the Department of Health Canada, which had a modern analytical laboratory.

Accordingly, in early May 1983, after speaking with Dr. Pierre Blais, a research scientist at the BMD who had a special interest in medical devices containing plastics and rubber, I bundled up and sent to the BMD samples of 3 different lots of the 50 mL syringes (B-D Plastipak, Becton-Dickinson of Rutherford, New Jersey) that I had in stock, identified by the syringe manufacturer's lot numbers. I asked whether any contaminants from these syringes could be responsible for the reactions in my patients. I had a feeling at the time that he wasn't completely surprised by what I described.

Within a few days, Dr. Blais, having used the BMD's state-of-the-art analytical laboratory, informed me that significant amounts of "a phenolic compound" had been found leaching into several different lots of IVP dyes that had been allowed to remain overnight in one of my syringes. He explained that the particular syringe lot in use at the time of the anaphylactic shock released three times as much contaminant, but all syringes leached some of this "phenolic compound" from the black rubber end of the syringe plunger.

When, by the middle of June, after repeated phone calls, I could extract no further specific information from the BMD's advanced analytical laboratory, I phoned the editor of the *Canadian Medical Association Journal (CMAJ)* and related my experience. The editor asked me to submit a letter to the journal, documenting my experience as a case report, and he would look at it. When I did so, on September 1, 1983, the editor exercised his editorial authority by publishing the article about the contamination of an X-ray dye by a "phenolic compound" from a natural rubber component of plastic syringes, identified by Health Canada's analytical laboratory at the Bureau of Medical devices in Ottawa.[1]

Disturbingly, in a following issue of the *CMAJ*, there was a letter from a London allergist, severely criticizing the "leap in logic" that implicated syringe rubber and "a phenolic compound" in this potentially fatal anaphylactic reaction associated with unsuspected contamination of X-ray dyes.

While I was still sombrely contemplating how to appropriately respond to this criticism, I received a phone call that would stand out as one of the high points in my medical career. It was Dr. Harry Fischer of Rochester, New York, who began by asking me if I knew who he was. Having already recognized his name and his soft Southern accent from hearing him speak about reactions to X-ray dye injections on two different occasions at large scientific meetings of North American radiologists (he was "one of the foremost international experts"[2] on X-ray dyes), and speaking as a diagnostic radiologist, I replied quietly, in a puzzled and somewhat meek tone: "Everyone knows Harry Fischer."

He said he had read my article in the *CMAJ* and stated that I had uncovered an important unconsidered aspect to the reactions encountered by radiologists injecting X-ray dyes. Then he took my breath away when he asked me to submit a similar case report to *Radiology* (the world's most prestigious journal in my specialty of diagnostic radiology). Dr. Fischer was *Radiology*'s editor in charge of papers on X-ray dyes, particularly concerning the adverse reactions associated with their injection into patients. He mentioned that he would write a commentary to accompany the article.

This was a remarkable honour, a request from an editor of a top international medical journal to submit a scientific paper, to someone practicing in a small private office, and who was just trying to do his best in the X-ray investigation of the patients entrusted to him.

Normally, about three to six months after submission of an article to a medical journal, one receives an airmail letter signifying its acceptance, or, much more commonly, its rejection. However, in this case, after about three months, I received another phone call from Dr. Fischer. In a very apologetic and somewhat embarrassed tone, he informed me that the other members of the editorial board had rejected the article, saying that the material had already been dealt with in another journal, the *CMAJ*.

When I put down the receiver, I was stunned, bewildered, disappointed and, most of all, deeply disturbed.

In essence, the events had unfolded in the following way. Dr. Fischer, an internationally recognized authority, and as already noted, the editor in charge of X-ray dye articles, had requested my short article on an unsuspected underlying contaminant that leached from a natural rubber component of disposable plastic syringes, as a cause of severe, potentially lethal reactions to the injections of these dyes — the dyes that were being used in IVPs, in dye studies of congenital heart disease, of coronary artery disease, and in arteriography for diseases of the blood supply to the limbs. This contamination implicated a type of syringe in almost universal use. Yet the requested article, which was on contamination from syringes used in an enormous number of injections of many different pharmaceuticals (including X-ray dyes) around the world — an article of vital interest to those performing the procedures and the patients receiving them — was blocked before it could enlighten U.S. radiologists, almost none of whom would have read the article in the *CMAJ*.

This left me brooding over how pressure had been exerted on the editorial board to prevent the disclosure of the contamination. Could interested companies really learn of the contents of articles when they have been submitted to the journal's editorial board, and then have the power to prevent their publication? Surely, this should be far outside the boundaries of ethical pharmaceutical corporate behaviour and the fundamental reason for the existence of medical journals.

It was almost a certainty that very few radiologists outside of Canada, with the notable exception of Dr. Fischer, would have read the article in the *CMAJ*. Thus, there was an imposed resistance to the dissemination of clinical evidence of the risk of this syringe rubber through the denial of the publication of an article authorized by their own editor, one of the world's most respected authorities on the subject.

The impact of these developments grew and boiled within me. My anger was not directed at Dr. Fischer, but at the other editors and at the syringe and pharmaceutical rubber manufacturers. In particular, I became furious at Health Canada's BMD, which appeared to be withholding information of vital importance to public health.

I had the most difficulty in understanding and justifying Health Canada's behaviour. Surely it would be unthinkable for a federal health protection agency to even consider withholding vital information from physicians about a contaminant that was imperiling the very lives of Canadian citizens. What could possibly motivate such a departure from their whole *raison d'être*? It must be emphasized that it was not just the lives of X-ray patients in Canada, but the lives of every person getting an injection of any pharmaceutical using disposable plastic syringes with natural rubber parts, which were in routine use across the world. Basic ethics demand that health protection bodies must keep themselves absolutely immune to any interference with the release of such vitally important information. Health protection agencies must not be manipulated by industries whose products have been proven to exhibit such profound negative public health potential.

Five

Concealing, Revealing, Then Inaction on the Hazardous Contamination of Medical Rubber MBT in Injected X-ray Dyes, Pharmaceuticals, Allergy Desensitization "Shots," IV Fluids, and Blood

After *Radiology*'s rejection of the article that Dr. Fischer had asked me to write, it took a few days of moping around before I could regroup and use the energy of anger to drive me towards an appropriate and sharply focused form of action.

Following much meditation, I decided to confront the Director of Health Canada's Bureau of Medical Devices in Ottawa, to ask him to justify the handling of this major public health issue.

Perhaps it was fortunate that the director was on holidays. The assistant director would speak to me. I explained how disappointed I was that a state-of-the-art analytical laboratory, established for the sole purpose of protecting our citizens from known hazards in medical devices, could only come up with an extremely generic term, "a phenolic compound" (an enormous group of organic chemicals that would include even the humble Aspirin), to describe a contaminant that could have killed my patient if immediate and appropriate treatment had not been instituted.

A sombre silence lingered on the line. Perhaps it was the sudden realization that the onus of the collective conscience of the Bureau of Medical Devices had been thrust onto his shoulders. I sensed the cold beads of sweat that must have been forming on his furrowed brow. I had the feeling that not only was he aware of the nature of the pharmaceutical rubber contamination, but perhaps I had touched on a very troubling and sensitive spot in his awareness of the behind-the-scenes developments — and the ultimate significance — of the revelations that were to follow.

Finally the silence was broken by these words, spoken in a muted monotone: "I'll have Dr. Pierre Blais phone you in a few minutes." Dr. Blais was the research scientist at the BMD who had a particular expertise in plastics and the natural rubbers being used in Canada's medical devices, but one whose actions and reports were controlled by the director of the laboratory. I sensed that a major breakthrough was about to take place in my quest for the cause of potentially lethal contamination of injections, one of which had occurred in a patient entrusted to me for an IVP.

Accordingly, in the middle of the busiest part of the office day, my secretary summoned me to say that a Dr. Pierre Blais from the Bureau of Medical Devices in Ottawa wished to speak to me.

I kept my patients, the X-ray technologists, and the secretarial staff waiting for over a half an hour as I listened to and then questioned Dr. Blais. I wrote down the specific details of the contamination that the laboratory at Health Canada's Bureau of Medical Devices had identified, coming from the natural rubber component of the disposable plastic syringes I had been using nine months ago, when my patient had suffered from an allergic anaphylactic shock. I asked for the exact nature and quantification of the eight different contaminants that were found to leach out the rubber components of the plastic syringes into the X-ray dye that I would inject. I recorded this information and phoned him again the next morning to confirm the exact details of this contamination that had been uncovered in early May 1983.

Thus, it was not until February 1984 that I was given the real meaning of "a phenolic compound" from a natural rubber contaminant that affected all three different lots of my syringes — a contamination that was potentially present in disposable syringes in universal use. A contamination that could have killed a patient who had been entrusted to me, not for treatment, but only for investigation.

Much later, in 1987, the BMD informed me that it was their standard practice to inform the manufacturers first about incidents such as MBT contamination, so that they would be prepared, to some extent, for the repercussions that would surely follow. As you have learned, the manufacturers were the only ones notified at the time of discovery. It was nine months later that Health Canada's BMD informed me of the true nature of the contaminants I had unknowingly injected into patients entrusted to me by referring doctors.

The syringe manufacturer (B-D, Becton-Dickinson) and the pharmaceutical rubber manufacturer (the West Rubber Company) were informed in May 1983 of the true nature of the contaminants, but I, who had sent the BMD my syringes for definitive analysis, was informed a full nine months after the event. I was told only because I had badgered them, and I received the laboratory report, not on the letterhead of the Bureau of Medical Devices, but only by phone!

As I have revealed, I was told, initially, that it was "a phenolic compound." These words cloaked MBT in a disguise that hid it from the prying eyes of anaphylaxis researchers. This is exactly comparable to a witness to a car accident who recognized the driver, wrote down the make, year, model, colour, and license plate number of the car involved, but who then withheld the defining details, telling the investigating police officer only that the victim was struck by some kind of vehicle.

It is inexplicable that, to this day, I have not received a written report of what was uncovered in a state of the art analytical laboratory, a Canadian government laboratory whose sole purpose was, and still is, to protect the health of Canadian citizens — but the syringe manufacturer and the West Rubber Company were notified promptly. I was left unable to notify the medical profession until August 1984, when the defining article was published in *Radiology*,[1] fifteen months after the manufacturers were informed.

Although the information (and misinformation) I received on the nature of the contamination were given to me by Dr. Blais, his actions in the laboratory, his phone communications with me — and his ultimate reports (verbal only) — were controlled by the Director of the Bureau of Medical Devices, who, fortunately it seems, had been away when I called to prevail on them to release the true nature of the contaminants. One must reach into the darkest depths of one's imagination to contemplate the motivation that was behind what seems to have been an attempt to conceal from the medical world — and from the large number of people globally at risk — the grave nature of such contamination of all injected pharmaceuticals. Yet the manufacturers were informed promptly! Why them and not us?

What might be seen as a strategic slant to this chain of events was created by the delay in the release of the true nature of the contaminants. The companies whose products were involved would be dealing only with old news, many months after the impact of a near-death situation.

The February 1984 verbal BMD report (from Dr. Pierre Blais) of the rubber contaminants found in May 1983 described as "a phenolic compound."

Substance	Amount (micrograms per mL)
mercaptobenzothiazole (MBT)	3
hydroxyethyl-mercaptobenzothiazole (H-MBT)	1.2
tertiary butyl–2-benzothiazole sulfaene amide	0.7
ethylene glycol	1.2
xylene	0.9
nonyl phenol	1.2
butyl hydroxytoluene	1.2
undefined phenol with an 8 carbon side chain	1.2

As I contemplated the results of the analysis, I became very disturbed at the enormity of what I had just learned. I kept staring at the list of chemical compounds, having no idea what most of them represented. I went home that night wondering how I should proceed.

Because I was dealing with a pharmaceutical, Dr. Bruce Gowdey, the professor who had taught me pharmacology in medical school, came to mind. Accordingly, the next day I called Dr. Gowdey at his office in the Department of Pharmacology at the University of Western Ontario, briefly told him my story and asked if he could offer any advice. He said he had jotted down my facts, while admitting he didn't know much about the compounds. He said that he would get back to me.

In a week, Dr. Gowdey walked into my office and handed me a manila folder with handwritten pages documenting what he had personally researched, an unbelievable amount of effort. Obviously, he felt it was his duty to become involved in what was a very great danger to public health.

Most notable in Dr. Gowdey's research was the organic compound mercaptobenzothiazole (MBT), a catalyst used in natural rubber manufacturing. His research revealed MBT to be an allergen, capable of causing allergic reactions and, as I discovered later, well known to the Canadian Worker's Compensation Board as a cause of allergic reactions in workers in industries using natural rubber, such as the tire industry. Benzothiazoles had been in use in rubber manufacturing since the late 1920s. A similar type of natural rubber, incorporating MBT and latex in manufacture, had been employed in the rubber stoppers for IV fluid and blood transfusion bottles for many years since that time.

After additional research, and armed with the corroborative journal article reprints in front of me, this time it was I who phoned Dr. Fischer. His voice projected a warm interest in hearing from me again. The sense of warmth changed to a grave, silent attentiveness as the significance of what I was relating sank in. The softness had vanished from his Southern accent as he asked me to revise my article, including this new information, and send it to him at his hospital address. There was an almost steely firmness, perhaps tempered with a touch of anger, as he said sharply, "I'll deal with this submission — personally!"

Accordingly, the article, "Contamination of Contrast Agents (X-ray dyes) by Rubber Components of 50 mL Disposable Syringes," appeared in the August 1984 edition of *Radiology*, accompanied by Dr. Fischer's commentary.[2]

In this way, the true nature of the "phenolic compound" was finally revealed to North American radiologists, in print in *Radiology*, one year and three months after it had been correctly identified to the involved companies by Health Canada's analytical laboratory at the Bureau of Medical Devices. The medical community at large, the dentists, nurses, and potential patients, remained uninformed of a widespread, potentially lethal threat.

It must be noted that this article contained information that — if it were acted on appropriately — would cause very great expense and difficulty for the West Rubber Company, the syringe manufacturers, and the pharmaceutical industry whose injectable drugs contained MBT natural rubber in ampoules and in unit dose syringes — worldwide. Regardless of these very large economic considerations, the great danger to public health should have demanded that they withdraw these natural-rubber-containing products as rapidly as possible, to prevent illness and many deaths across the world from syringe-mediated allergic reactions to MBT contaminants of injections.

I was a diagnostic radiologist who was injecting only one pharmaceutical, an X-ray dye — not a family doctor, or an internal medicine specialist, who would be administering several different drugs in a day, using disposable plastic syringes. Unquestionably, the anaphylactic shock drama that had taken place in my office in early May 1983 must have been representative of many serious reactions, with deaths being repeated throughout the world. The same risk was present whenever and wherever an injection was being performed using a disposable plastic syringe, almost all of which had MBT-latex natural rubber plunger parts, causing many cases of anaphylactic shock and many deaths, but there was only one case that had been attributed to an allergic reaction to a contaminant in an injection — MBT.

Some severe reactions encountered were truly allergic reactions to the pharmaceutical being injected, but MBT is a fairly strong allergen and would have caused most of them. Latex allergy, too, would have been responsible for some of the severe reactions associated with natural rubber with injected pharmaceuticals or fluids. The reactions and deaths were invariably blamed on allergy to the local anesthetic, the antibiotic, the insulin, the immunization vaccine, or other pharmaceutical being injected, because of the of the unawareness that MBT (and latex) had contaminated the injections.

It is pertinent to note that in 1981, Petersen's group in Australia proved that syringes made by the Japanese manufacturer Terumo leached an MBT compound, H-MBT, into the syringe contents.[3] H-MBT exhibited a poisoning effect on living human cells. The group showed that MBT compounds were responsible for the deaths of cells when certain disposable plastic syringes were used to extract or deposit samples of these cells being grown in cultures in laboratories around the world. MBT compounds were toxic to embryos and showed cancer-causing potential in the laboratory.[4]

The HMBT caused a high spike in electrophoresis blood chemistry graphs in the same area where hydrocortisone and betamethasone blood levels were being measured, "resulting in an overestimate of drug concentrations." They showed that other electrophoresis drug blood levels were similarly interfered with.

The amount of MBT contamination was related to the length of time the contents remained in the syringes and to the caliber of the barrels (not the volume of fluid in the syringe). This caused them to comment that "The inadvertent administration" of MBT compounds "may be of particular importance in hospitalized infants, especially premature infants, children, and patients with impaired elimination."

Glass syringes showed no leaching at all, but two brands of disposable syringes with natural rubber plunger seals showed significant leaching of MBT compounds. Petersen warned: "This situation clearly has the potential to compromise the conclusions drawn from the pharmacokinetic and therapeutic monitoring data, with possible implications for clinical management." The reader should take particular note of this prescient observation in 1981 regarding children (both regarding toxicity and in causing falsely high assays of drugs) as the story unfolds.

The toxic effects of this MBT contaminant were shown only in a laboratory setting. However, realizing that this toxicity must apply equally to human patients who are composed of many millions of similar cells and, to protect these numerous patients — and to protect its reputation as an honorable and forthright company — Terumo announced the danger of the MBT contamination to the medical profession in an article in the *Australia and New Zealand Medical Journal*.[5] Terumo made sure that the quality control of the rubber manufacturing was increased at the factory to minimize the MBT risk, while they worked on developing an MBT-free replacement for the syringe plunger tips. In 1985 Terumo replaced the plunger tips with a new synthetic rubber that didn't require MBT or latex in manufacture (a safety measure that was not followed by other manufacturers for years).

I believed that immediate measures necessary to protect patients would be taken (as Terumo had felt obligated to begin doing in 1981) firstly by the North American manufacturers and secondly by government health regulatory bodies. All of us have a right to expect an adherence to such fundamental principles of ethics and public health.

Although, initially, I was not informed of the true nature of "the phenolic compound" found by the Bureau of Medical devices, it was a rule that the BMD would notify both the manufacturers and their FDA counterparts in the U.S. of any significant safety issues they uncovered.

Thus, I believe that it was no coincidence that on May 23, 1983, Harry M. Meyer, the Director of the National Center for Drugs and Biologics in the U.S. Department of Health and Human Services (this would have been after the BMD had analyzed my syringes at the beginning of May and notified the FDA) sent a notice to "assure that all manufacturers of parenteral products and closure manufacturers are informed about recent pertinent findings." This meant the presence of 2-MCBT (MBT) leaching into syringe and ampoule contents from natural rubber contact. On the other hand, the medical, dental, and nursing professions, who would be involved in the recognition and treatment of severe reactions, were kept in the dark about this prevalent menace, totally unaware of MBT contamination.[6] The following is a copy of that letter of notification:

DEPARTMENT OF HEALTH AND HUMAN SERVICES

May 23, 1983

Dear Registrant:

The National Center for Drugs and Biologics (NCDB), Food and Drug Administration (FDA) is constantly concerned about **undesirable substances** that may leach from plastic and glass containers and from their closures into drugs or biologic products after filling. The purpose of this notification is to assure that all manufacturers of **parenteral products and closure manufacturers are informed about recent pertinent findings**.

Two years ago M.C. Petersen, et al. published a report on "Leaching of 2-(Hydroxyethylmercapto) benzothiazole into contents of disposable syringes" (J. Pharm. Sci. 70: 1139–1142, 1981). The compound was believed to result from a reaction between 2-mercaptobenzothiazole (2-MCBT), a rubber vulcanization accelerator present in the rubber plunger seal, and ethylene oxide used for sterilization of the syringes. At the recent APhA meeting, the subject of physical-chemical rubber related interactions was discussed in a session on Small Volume Parenteral Packaging. **Several lots of different drugs packaged for single dose delivery syringes were analyzed by the National Center for Drug Analysis. Testing showed the presence of 2-MCBT** in low concentration 4–8 ppm). The source of the 2-MCBT was the rubber plunger-seal and the rubber sheath meant to cover the needle. Such extraneous matter in the product may interfere with drug potency assays and may constitute a health hazard to the recipients of the product. The compound is being **evaluated** currently as a **suspect carcinogen** by the National Toxicological Program in a chronic study in mice and rays, but the **results will not be known until late 1983.**

Irrespective of its toxicity profile, whenever extraneous substances are identified in drugs or biologics products, corrective measures should be taken to the extent possible and reasonable. **All manufacturers of injectable human drug and biological products now in containers with rubber closures formulated with 2-MCBT should implement a program to test these products for the presence of 2-MCBT.** If the substance is detected consideration should be given to replacing the closure. The most prudent action would be to use another closure that is not made with 2-MCBT. **The NCDB knows of one firm that has already begun replacing the closures for all of their injectable products with 2-MCBT-free rubber closures.**

In the selection of other closure formulations, testing should be carried out so that the potential problems with other leachable substances are avoided.

Please advise the NCDB of any additional information you may have on this subject and the plans you may have to detect and control the presence of 2-MCBT in your injectable products. Drug manufacturers should respond to the Associate Director for Compliance, Office of Drugs, and biologics manufacturers to the Director, Division of Compliance, Office of Biologics.

Sincerely yours,

Harry M. Meyer, Jr., M.D.
Director
National Center for Drugs and Biologics

Note, particularly, that MBT is the centrepiece of this warning and that the increasingly popular unit dose syringes were being singled out — as early as May 1983 — in this Health and Human Services document.

One thing the reader must take particular note of is it was compulsory that manufacturers (syringe and pharmaceutical manufacturers) be alerted with a similar notice, also in 1983, when Reepmeyer and Juhl discovered MBT leaching from rubber into the contents of unit-dose syringes.[7] It is unfortunate that only the rubber manufacturers and the pharmaceutical industry received Dr. Meyer's MBT warning and that only radiologists would have read the 1984 article in *Radiology*. The following two paragraphs from the *Radiology* article would have justifiably disturbed the medical, dental, and nursing professions and the general public, if they had been informed of this danger. The revelations in the article should have made the manufacturers take immediate action to eliminate this toxic and allergenic threat, with the greatest haste possible:

> If bad lots of rubber components of 50 mL syringes have been manufactured, then in warehouses and hospital storerooms and shelves across North America, a Pandora's box of chemical and biochemical substances are awaiting release into contrast agents when syringes are filled and left loaded for any period of time.
>
> If these rubber parts are indeed capable of contaminating our contrast agents, there would be, also, **a much more widespread similar problem resulting from the rubber caps sealing vials of many different pharmaceuticals (including contrast agents, antibiotics, other drugs, and even water for injection)**, rendering these agents toxic and/or allergenic, or even less potent. Have the results of allergy testing been made questionable in some cases by (a) using syringes with rubber components and (b) by keeping allergens in rubber-capped vials? Should there be a fairly general return to all-glass ampoules for injectables?
>
> – From *Radiology* (1984), Volume 152, pages 539–40

Not the least important aspect of this MBT exposure was the natural rubber seals of ampoules. Also of particular importance was MBT's presence in the rubber in the plunger tips of the unit dose syringes, which were loaded with an exact dose of a pharmaceutical, and often with expiry dates of three years after manufacture. Throughout this time the natural rubber would be in intimate contact with the pharmaceutical to be injected. As Reepmeyer and Juhl discovered in 1981, 50 percent of all unit-dose disposable syringes tested in their FDA laboratory showed significant MBT contamination. These unit dose syringes were being promoted as a superior method of administering pharmaceuticals because they greatly reduced the chance of errors in dose administration.[8]

The reasons for, and mechanisms behind the directorate of the BMD issuing (orally) an assay report that the MBT compounds they identified were an ill defined "phenolic compound" will, no doubt, be examined in the future so that this scenario does not occur ever again. The only beneficiaries of the concealment of the true nature of the contaminants would be the manufacturers. Only they were informed of the true MBT nature of the contamination at the time of the "phenolic compound" report.

Following the discovery of the syringe rubber contamination of my X-ray dyes, further research uncovered that a Danish company, Pharmaplast, made more expensive all-plastic syringes. Having no natural rubber parts, the Pharmaplast syringes were free from the allergens, MBT, and latex. Although the performance of these syringes was not quite as good as the ones I had been using, I found a Canadian distributor and started to use Pharmaplast syringes exclusively. (In 1987, I found a Canadian distributor of MBT-free Terumo syringes which were even more satisfactory for my needs, and I continued to use these syringes exclusively for the remainder of my career.)

I continued my rapid IVP injection technique, taking comfort in the belief that, by selecting MBT-free, natural-rubber-free Pharmaplast syringes, and by appropriately notifying the health protection authorities, my injections no longer should be accompanied by a life-threatening danger of the exposure of my patients to natural rubber allergens, MBT, and latex. I was confident, similarly, that natural rubber seals would have been eliminated from the billion or more pharmaceutical ampoules on pharmacy and hospital supply shelves and in warehouses across the world.

Six

A Preventable Repeat Performance

In 1986, three and a half years after recognizing that my patients had been exposed to allergenic MBT through my IVP dye injections, I once again started to get a feeling that a few more than usual of my IVP patients were developing hives and that the facial flushing was somewhat more pronounced. Suddenly, in a déjà vu type of experience, one of my patients went into shock immediately following a dye injection.

Again, treatment was instituted as the patient's pulse rate rose, and the pulse pressure dropped dramatically, with the pulse finally becoming imperceptible. An adrenaline injection, a large dose of intravenous cortisone, and oxygen by mask kept the patient alive (although without a palpable pulse) until the ambulance crew arrived, transporting her to a nearby hospital emergency department within 30 minutes of the onset of this life-threatening anaphylactic shock event. Again, one of my patients survived a potentially fatal allergic episode without complications.

I knew that this dreaded form of allergic reaction should not be due to the presence of MBT from my syringes, because there were no natural rubber components in the Danish Pharmaplast syringes. I also knew that the rubber-like seals on the glass ampoules should not have been made from natural latex rubber, using MBT as a catalyst, because health protection authorities in Australia, Canada, and the U.S., and the pharmaceutical rubber manufacturers, had been informed of the danger three and a half years earlier, not only about MBT's capability of inducing life-threatening allergic reactions, but its significant toxicity to cells and to the developing fetus.[1,2,3,4,5,6] Nonetheless, I suspected that, somehow, natural rubber containing MBT and latex had been used in the ampoule seals of the IVP dye being used (Conray 400, 68 percent sodium iothalamate, manufactured by Mallinckrodt).

I was deeply concerned that I might be faced again with the withholding — or the significant delay in sending — the results of the analysis of the dye lot associated with this episode of anaphylaxis. My previous experience was still burned into my memory.

Once again, I called the OMA's Adverse Drug Reporting centre for the names of government testing laboratories.

As a result of the OMA's advice, a decision was made to send samples of the Conray 400 X-ray dye ampoules, not just to one, but to three different government analytical laboratories. Notably, one of these was the laboratory of the Centre for Forensic Sciences, whose motto is "*scientia pro justicia*" ("science for justice"), a fitting motto for the situation at hand. By registered mail, I sent ampoules of the dye lot in use to the three different laboratories, asking specifically for assays for MBT contamination, stating that I strongly suspected that the manufacturer, Mallinckrodt, had used natural rubber seals on the ampoules of the X-ray dye — and that this rubber had been manufactured with MBT as a vulcanization catalyst.

In one week, all three laboratories reported the same three things: 1) the ampoules were indeed sealed with natural rubber, 2) significant amounts of MBT were found contaminating the dye in each ampoule, and 3) they had sliced up the natural rubber seals and proven that MBT could be extracted from all of these seals.

Until that time, I had been injecting these dyes with a comfortable feeling that the natural rubber/MBT contamination had been resolved and that my patients were no longer at risk of MBT anaphylaxis. The three and a half years that had elapsed since my last episode of MBT contamination-caused anaphylaxis should have been adequate to eliminate the MBT problem, but this episode was proof that this potentially lethal menace was being allowed to continue as an unsuspected allergenic and toxic contaminant of injected pharmaceuticals, IV fluids, and blood transfusions. Health Canada's failure to eliminate natural rubber, with its known MBT and latex allergens, was indefensible, especially since MBT was a known toxin as well.

During my conversations at this time with the Bureau of Medical Devices, I learned that it was standard procedure at the BMD to first inform manufacturers of important findings, such as the occurrence of MBT leaching into their injectable products, so that there would be adequate time for the companies to brace themselves for the aftermath of such revelations and to prepare some kind of explanation. This admission was proof to me that, in 1983, the manufacturers had been alerted to the true nature of the MBT contamination of my X-ray dye many months before I was. For some reason, I was notified nine months later of this "phenolic compound." My notification had only come after repeated requests for specific details of the contamination, but all the while MBT remained hidden behind the generic "phenolic compound" smokescreen.

In defiance of accepted public health principles, the MBT contamination of injections was allowed to continue.

Pharmaceutical rubber continued to be manufactured with MBT and latex, and the unit dose syringes with natural rubber seals continued in production, still being filled at the factory with carefully measured doses of pharmaceuticals — a much-promoted (and much more expensive) method of administration of pharmaceuticals.

The enormity of the natural rubber contamination of injections with MBT and latex is staggering. An insight into its magnitude can be found in an article by F.M. Keim, an executive of the West Rubber Company, a major world supplier of natural rubber products for pharmaceutical companies and syringe manufacturers. He stated that if all the small natural rubber sealing caps on pharmaceutical ampoules manufactured by the West Rubber Company in one year, 1977, were placed end to end, they would stretch around the world three times.[7] The West Rubber Company was a large corporation, only one of many manufacturers around the world making natural rubber, using MBT and latex, for pharmaceutical vial seals.

This was not even considering that (along with the natural rubber seals of pharmaceutical vials that Keim referred to) to inject these pharmaceuticals, plastic syringes with natural rubber plunger tips were being used, compounding the risk of leaching. Furthermore, natural rubber "corks" were in universal use in inverted IV and blood transfusion bottles, with virtually no one attributing the anaphylactic reactions to the rubber. This pharmaceutical rubber was destined to be in contact with drugs and fluids, often for prolonged periods, before being injected.

Keim's comment was intended to impress the reader with how much West Rubber Company natural rubber was being produced for the pharmaceutical industry at that time. I mention it only to emphasize the vast scope of the exposure of patients to allergenic latex and to MBT, which is both allergenic — capable of causing the full range of allergic reactions, including life-threatening anaphylactic shock and edema of the larynx — and is well-known to be toxic, carcinogenic (cancer-inducing) and teratogenic (capable of damaging the developing foetus).

Thus, there was a pervasive presence of MBT/latex natural rubber in contact with pharmaceuticals destined for injection. In 1981, the FDA's National Center for Drug Analysis proved that 50 percent of this natural rubber contaminated the injectable contents of disposable syringes in unit-dose form with MBT.[8]

However, MBT's prevalence as a contaminant of injections was so suppressed that in the medical literature of the whole world, there have been only two reports of anaphylaxis from MBT exposure through contamination of injections. These reports were not from a large, eminent university teaching center, such as in Toronto, Montreal, Boston, Paris, London or Tokyo. These two isolated reports, at a three and a half year interval, came from my small private radiology office in London, Ontario, in 1984 and again 1987 — where only one pharmaceutical was being injected, an X-ray dye. In the first case, a cause was searched for and found, MBT; in the second reported case in 1987, the presence of allergenic MBT was predicted before it was found as a contaminant of the X-ray dye by the three Canadian government analytical laboratories.

Elsewhere, across the world, the many anaphylactic reactions and deaths were not being attributed to MBT, because no one was aware of its presence as a contaminant. Erroneously and invariably, these allergic reactions were attributed to the pharmaceutical being injected (e.g. the local anesthetic, the X-ray dye, the insulin, the antibiotic, etc.).

Because of its worldwide prevalence, anaphylactic-shock-producing contamination of injections by the toxic allergen MBT should have made headlines in newspapers around the world, and whole issues of medical journals should have been devoted to this threat, but it was more than just soft-pedalled. It was allowed to fade (perhaps, even more likely, it was *made* to fade) into the background of medical knowledge and the consciousness of diagnosticians. Many millions, or perhaps billions, of ampoule doses of pharmaceuticals contaminated with MBT and latex — and the innumerable natural-rubber-containing disposable syringes around the world — were knowingly (by manufacturers and health "protection" agencies) allowed to be used up on unsuspecting patients receiving injections from unsuspecting doctors, dentists, and nurses, often in hospitals that were believed to be free from natural rubber exposure to patients (latex-free hospitals).

At that time, the allergy desensitizing regimes in use for patients suffering from recurrent asthmatic attacks from identified allergens deserve particular scrutiny. In my 1955 to 1957 internal medicine internship, I was fortunate to come under the instruction of Dr. John Toogood, one of Canada's foremost allergists of the time. He taught that when patients were being desensitized to allergens via repeated small doses of subcutaneous injections with very dilute solutions of these allergens, when a new replacement ampoule of allergenic material was started, there would be a significant risk of anaphylactic shock with the first dose of the new allergy desensitizing preparation. The accepted reasoning was that the violent allergic reactions were due to variations in the concentrations of the biological materials. The concentration of these biological preparations could not be calibrated as accurately as pure chemicals, resulting in patients being at risk of receiving a far higher concentration of desensitizing allergens than anticipated, with an attendant greater risk of a severe reaction.

A very significant variable was not being factored in. The vials had quite large natural rubber caps, to permit repeated puncturing by needles as desensitizing doses were being extracted for the subcutaneous injections ("allergy shots," as they are called). Just as was the case with the rubber components of syringes, the rubber caps sealing off the new allergy shot ampoules were made from different batches of natural rubber. Thus, there were variable amounts of MBT leaching into the contents of different ampoules, depending on a particular rubber batch.

Allergy to any MBT (or latex) that was present as a contaminant of the allergy shot was, therefore, a major consideration in the incidence of anaphylaxis attacks whenever desensitizing material was taken from a new ampoule. As already stated, in 1981 the FDA's National Center for Drug Analysis showed that 50 percent of pharmaceutical rubber leached significant amounts of MBT. This referred to unit dose syringes, despite the fact that they had less surface contact with the injected material than many other commonly used disposable syringes.

All people are players in this puppet show called Life. We all have our strings attached. However, we come equipped with the scissors of conscience that can be used to cut us free, allowing us to be not only independent thinkers, but, as physicians, the ethical performers we promised to be when we took the Hippocratic Oath. (Some individuals' scissors are allowed to become more blunt than others — and some of the strings are tempered to be much tougher, and thus are more tenacious.) We rightly expect government bodies entrusted with public health protection to operate with no strings attached and must, absolutely, never be manipulated like marionettes. They must never even be suspected of being under the control of corporations, which may place profits far above public health issues. Otherwise, there would be no purpose in having such bodies; a much smaller private industry would be capable of doing much better, and at a far lower cost to the taxpayer.

Even after the finding by the National Center for Drug Analysis concerning MBT compounds leaching into the contents of medical syringes,[9] much of Europe, and all of North America continued to use natural (latex) rubber, in syringes and intravenous apparatus, but the quality control of rubber manufacturing obviously (and understandably) was increased substantially in 1982 to 1983, to lessen the magnitude of the MBT exposure that in 1981 had been defined as a toxin in Australia[10] and as a common contaminant of pharmaceuticals in the U.S.[11] This increase in quality control after 1981 would account for the cessation of reports of cell deaths in human cell cultures. The significant toxicity of MBT compounds that severely damaged the cell wall membranes must have been affecting patients in 1981, particularly small infants, since similar size syringes were used for all patients. This would have had particular importance in babies requiring repeated injections, such as those that were seriously ill in hospitals.

The improved quality control that would have occurred around 1982, fostered by the Reepmeyer and by the Terumo syringe experiences, would have had only a slight effect on the incidence of anaphylactic shock from MBT-contaminated injections, because only trace amounts of an allergen are necessary to trigger a cascading anaphylactic shock allergic reaction. It must be said, however, that a significant reduction in the amount of MBT leaching would have had a large influence on the toxicological impact of natural rubber in contact with injectables after 1982 — a feature and a timing that will have significant additional implications in the second part of this story.

Seven

Inaction on Rubber Contamination Leaching Into Pharmaceuticals Worldwide

The well-known danger of natural MBT-latex-rubber should have resulted in government health protection agencies universally outlawing all medical components that allow rubber contact with any injectable (intravenous, intramuscular, intracutaneous, or subcutaneous) drugs or fluids.

It is common knowledge that many hospitals have declared themselves free from exposing staff and patients to natural rubber (e.g. latex-free hospitals). While declaring themselves latex-free, it is obvious that all of their patients, repeatedly, were being exposed to natural rubber (MBT-latex-rubber), not by skin contact, not by the oral ingestion route, but by the much more dangerous systemic route (through injections), using disposable plastic syringes containing natural rubber, through the rubber seals on drug ampoules and, particularly, through the triple threat of rubber containing parts of IV and blood transfusion apparatus (large rubber stoppers of inverted glass bottles, rubber side lines for injecting medications, and rubber float valves).

Despite all that Health Canada knew about the potentially fatal allergic reactions and the toxicity issues related to MBT starting at least in 1983, they issued the following toothless announcement in 1989 — which left the enforcement up to the manufacturers:[1]

APRIL 1989

NOTES NO. 11
LEACHATES IN INJECTABLE DRUGS

The Health Protection Branch has continuing concern over the leaching of toxic substances into drugs from closures and other packaging components used in the injectable drug containers and administration devices. Of particular concern are the residues from substances used as accelerators in the manufacture of certain rubbers, specifically; nitrosamines, **2- mercaptobenzothiazole (2-MCBT, 2-MBT)** and related substances. C.01.069(a) of the Food and Drug Regulations requires that the immediate container of a drug prepared for parenteral injection shall be of such material and construction that no deleterious substance is yielded to the contents thereof. Furthermore, Division 2 of Part C of the Food and Drug Regulations (Good Manufacturing Practices) requires that packaging materials and finished products be tested against established specifications (C.02.016 and C.02.018), and that drugs in their packages be tested for stability

(C.02.028). Compliance with these regulations requires that during product development, tests and specifications be developed to ensure that hazardous substances are not leached into the drug during the shelf life of the product or under the recommended conditions of use. The Health Protection Branch considers that rubber containing **leachable toxic substances (including 2-MCBT, 2-MBT)** and nitrosamines or which are likely to form such substances **are unacceptable** for use in packaging components and administration devices in direct contact with injectable drugs.

Compliance with the Regulations will be assessed during the premarket review and during CMP inspections.

This was only a "Note" sent to rubber manufacturing companies and to syringe and pharmaceutical manufacturers, specifically warning about MBT leaching. Of particular and disturbing significance is that it was not sent to the medical, dental, nursing, or veterinary professions — and was not published in newspapers where patients would be alerted. Notes No. 11 discloses that Health Canada was fully aware that injectable drugs were allowed to remain on the market in contact with natural rubber parts. It even documents that they understood that this rubber leached toxic/allergenic MBT (as well as latex) into the injected fluids. It was a Health Canada laboratory (Bureau of Medical Devices in Ottawa) that had proven allergenic MBT contamination from MBT-latex-rubber had caused anaphylactic shock on two separate occasions in my office, when only one pharmaceutical was being injected (the radiopaque X-ray dye).

While admitting that this was "unacceptable," instead of absolutely banning the use of natural MBT-latex rubber, they only *assessed* "compliance with regulations" ... "during the pre-market review and during CMP inspections."

Understandably, this might raise the question of what purpose was being served by this government body. They leave Canadian citizens exposed to known — and preventable lethal risks. The choice of words likes "toxic," "noxious," and "unacceptable" demonstrates, clearly, that they understood that MBT contamination is capable of causing illness and death. They continue to abandon their very *raison d'être* – implicit in the words "Health Protection Branch." Just whom are they protecting?

We are all aware that lobbying goes on behind the scenes to protect corporate interests, but what we are discussing here is a failure to act — an inexcusable permissiveness — resulting in unnecessary severe reactions and deaths, not just in North America, but also throughout the world.[2]

Known Allergy Risk from Intravenous, Subcutaneous, and Intramuscular Injections

In a letter dated May 1, 1990, Judi Weissinger, Assistant Director (Pharmacology/Toxicology) at the Office of Drug Evaluation II of the FDA in Rockville, Maryland, answered my request for information on the possibility that natural rubber was still being allowed to come in contact with injected pharmaceuticals and intravenous fluids in the U.S.[3]

Remember, 1990 was nine years after the FDA's own National Center for Drug Analysis showed widespread MBT contamination of drugs from natural rubber, nine years after Australian researchers identified MBT from syringes as being toxic to human cells, and seven years after they were alerted to syringe rubber as the source of allergenic MBT anaphylaxis from an injection of an X-ray dye.

This is an excerpt from her reply to my letter:

> We (the FDA) currently are **not approving** drug products contained in syringes with rubber-tipped plungers or rubber closures containing MBT leachables for use with solutions for intravenous injection. When additional information regarding the hypersensitivity and **reproductive teratology** are available, a decision will be made regarding the safe use of rubber containing MBT leachables. At that time, allowable levels of leachables will be specified, or **we will take steps to effect discontinuation** of rubber syringe plunger tips and rubber stoppers synthesized with **2-MBT** accelerator for use with drugs.

Because this letter is from a high-ranking American FDA official, it is particularly disturbing. The FDA was banning nothing. Only drugs in unit-dose syringes that were meant for intravenous use were "no longer being approved" — and those already manufactured were being left on the market. In many cases the natural rubber content was not even disclosed on the packaging.[4] What is even more important, in spite of the proven dangers of natural (latex-MBT) rubber coming in contact with pharmaceuticals, the local anesthetics, insulin, vaccines, and other pharmaceuticals, which were destined for subcutaneous or intramuscular injection, were not affected by this directive and were often dispensed as unit dose syringes (with up to three years of rubber/drug contact before use) — and these could still be manufactured.

The significant risk of anaphylactic shock and death from these injections was being completely ignored. The admission that MBT was known to induce abnormalities in the developing fetus ("reproductive teratology") — while not banning MBT contamination of injections — is reprehensible. MBT-latex-rubber may be a major preventable cause of birth defects!

The letter lays bare the almost inert and truly unacceptable behaviour of a major health protection agency — knowingly permitting the continued exposure of U.S. citizens to an unsuspected toxic, allergenic, and teratogenic (damaging to the developing fetus) substance whenever an intramuscular, intracutaneous, or subcutaneous injection was administered. As early as 1981, the FDA referred to MBT's known allergenicity, toxicity, and its cancer-causing potential.[5]

Pertinent Medical Facts Regarding MBT-latex-rubber Manufacturing

Health Canada's Dr. Pierre Blais, who'd had a major research interest in pharmaceutical rubber and plastics, was a key player in the study of medical devices containing rubber and plastics at the Bureau of Medical Devices in Ottawa. In this role, he wrote a chapter in *Quality Assurance in Pharmaceuticals Manufactured in Hospitals* (1985), describing that rubber is manufactured in batches, quite similar to mixing up a batch of bread dough or a batch of cookies. Even when the batch is considered to be thoroughly mixed, there are commonly pockets of the unchanged components of the original mechanical mixture.

Notwithstanding the melting that occurs when a batch of natural rubber is being heated and some of the constituents blend in solution, foci of the substances mixed into the particular batch of rubber remain unchanged — insidiously. Some, like MBT, are leachable into injectable fluids and pharmaceuticals when such MBT-latex-rubber is used in the manufacture of syringes, ampoules, or intravenous administration equipment. It is exactly this feature that always should have made natural rubber absolutely unacceptable for medical applications that allow contact with injected drugs and injected IV fluids (including blood transfusions). Even skin contact with rubber can cause anaphylaxis. However, it is always latex that is blamed for such allergic reactions — because of total unawareness of the MBT that is an essential part of the rubber manufacturing process (vulcanization).

In my two clusters of injection-related allergic reactions, MBT-latex rubber was always present, but *only when MBT leaching was proven to be present did the clusters arise*. Thus, although latex has the potential to cause some allergic reactions and anaphylaxis, MBT appears to be the predominant allergenic factor. It is for this reason that the term MBT-latex-rubber should be used whenever natural rubber is being discussed.

Even the rubber inflatable enema tips, used for barium enemas in the practice of diagnostic radiology, have resulted in severe anaphylactic reactions, including deaths — and that was just from mucosal surface contact — not from the much more dangerous systemic (injection) route.[6,7]

MBT (mercapto-benzothiazole) has been used as a vulcanization catalyst (accelerator) since the late 1920s and has long been recognized as an allergen in rubber manufacturing industries, like tire manufacturing.[8] This is the reason MBT is included routinely in skin tests of rubber industry workers being investigated for allergic reactions.

In 1969, Guess and O'Leary, Australian pharmacology researchers, studied the toxicology of MBT in a laboratory setting. They were aware that MBT was being used extensively in the manufacture of natural rubber, which was being incorporated into disposable syringes and in pharmaceutical rubber, as seals for drug ampoules, in disposable syringes, and in parts of intravenous and transfusion administration sets.

They proved that MBT could damage cell walls and this damage could progress to cell wall rupture (cell lysis). Furthermore, they showed that MBT was a cumulative toxin, increasing in concentration with repeated injections, and that it was particularly toxic to the liver, causing toxic hepatitis. They warned, ominously, that MBT compounds posed a particular risk to children because adults and children are treated using syringes of similar size, with children receiving a far higher relative dose of leached MBT compounds.

They noted that MBT compounds were not eliminated in the urine. They attributed this to MBT becoming bound to the proteins in the blood (plasma proteins). Healthy kidney tubules do not allow large protein molecules to be excreted in the urine, thus allowing MBT compounds to accumulate to higher concentrations in the body with repeated exposure from contaminated injections.

Allergists have long recognized that when drugs become bound to plasma proteins, this drug-protein complex (hapten-protein complex) can be treated as a foreign protein against which the body develops antibodies. In allergic patients, when the body's antibodies react with any foreign protein (be it shellfish protein or MBT-protein complex) there can be massive release of histamine-like substances from the body, resulting in a profound drop in blood pressure, with a significant risk of death if not treated promptly — and correctly.

In 1981, Petersen's group of Australian researchers knew that MBT (mercaptobenzothiazole), an essential catalyst in the manufacturing process of vulcanization, and its sterilization byproduct, H-MBT (hydroxyethyl-MBT), were both known to be toxic and allergenic. They were proven to leach out of the rubber components of disposable medical syringes, killing human cells in laboratory cultures. The H-MBT is formed when MBT is exposed to the ethylene oxide gas that is commonly used to sterilize syringes. The Australian medical profession, the syringe and rubber manufacturers, were all notified in 1981. This information would have been shared with health protection agencies in the U.K., the U.S., and Canada at the same time.

Again in 1981, as already noted, the National Center for Drug Analysis found that natural rubber components of medical disposable syringes (unit-dose syringes, in particular, were studied) leached significant amounts of MBT compounds into the pharmaceutical being injected.[9] This discovery has great significance. The Guess and O'Leary experiments in 1969 showed MBT's potential for cumulative toxicity, because it became bound to human proteins in the bloodstream.[10]

Meek and Pettit suggested MBT as a major factor in the unexplained development of liver damage in premature infants on continuous intravenous feeding.[11] Infant feeding infusion pumps often use large 50 mL syringes with large rubber plunger parts. These syringes are often larger than the size of a premature infant's thigh. Meek and Pettit proved that the amount of MBT leaching was directly related to the surface area of the rubber part in contact with the fluid or drug in the syringe, or ampoule.

In 1983, a series of reactions to X-ray dye injections in my office, including a life-threatening anaphylactic shock, were proven to be related to MBT contamination from the disposable syringes being used.[12] As already stated, the syringe manufacturers, rubber manufacturers, and the medical profession were alerted.

It is axiomatic, therefore, that it was unacceptable for natural rubber to be allowed to come in contact with anything being injected, intravenously, intramuscularly, or subcutaneously. There can be no other rational or ethical way of considering the consequences of knowingly exposing injections of pharmaceuticals and fluids to natural rubber contact.

Yet in 1987, in a second series of increased reactions to X-ray dye injections in my office in London, Ontario, another of my patients experienced an anaphylactic shock episode, again proven to be associated with MBT contamination of the dye. In 2005, a disturbing document was published regarding the persistence of the MBT-latex-rubber hazard in injected pharmaceuticals. The article was by a group of researchers from Johns Hopkins University,[13] noting that it was estimated that "20 percent of pharmaceutical vials manufactured contained natural rubber" and that it wasn't mandatory to specify the natural rubber content. The article stated, "Presently, the pharmacist must contact the pharmaceutical company or perform a visual inspection to determine the composition of vial closures."

They describe how "the dry, molded, natural rubber used in the packaging of medical devices" created "an allergenic exposure risk for latex-allergic individuals who receive parenteral medications." The allergenic reactions were assigned to latex because MBT was virtually unmentionable as an allergen.

Pharmaceuticals are not considered to be allergenic unless they become bound to plasma proteins. In 1969[14] and in 1985,[15] the cumulative nature of MBT compound toxicity was related to their becoming protein-bound in the blood, making elimination through normal kidneys impossible (the kidneys only pass protein in the urine when kidney damage is present, and this is the reason doctors routinely test urine for proteins).

When medications bind to our plasma proteins, in allergic types of individuals, the body may recognize this drug-protein complex ("hapten-protein" complex, as allergy researchers call this feature) as a foreign protein, and develop antibodies to it. In these patients, when the antibodies combine with this "foreign protein," there is a release of large amounts of histamine-like substances, which causes any combination of flushing, hives, laryngeal oedema, anaphylactic shock, and death, in the same way that exposure to shellfish does in some people.

The MBT/natural rubber hazard existed wherever pharmaceuticals were injected — and even can be found today — still unsuspected by the nurses, doctors, or dentists injecting and the patients receiving the injections, still permitted by "health protection" government bodies, and still virtually unmentioned in the annals of allergy.

One can use Google to research, entering such terms as "latex in vaccine packaging," "pre-filled syringes/natural rubber," "local anesthetic cartridges/latex allergy," perhaps prefacing these searches with "dentistry," or "veterinary medicine," since these writings appear to yield success in finding articles. This will uncover that MBT-latex-natural rubber is still being used in many vaccines, some local anesthetics, and some insulin unit-dose syringes.

In a July 2008 U.S. Government Centers for Disease Control document, 28 vaccines are listed with natural rubber seals in contact with the vaccine. This government document can be downloaded from the Internet. After all you have been reading about the hazards of MBT/latex natural rubber in contact with injections, in Canada, the B.C. Centre for Disease Control released this chart in January 2009, displaying the utter failure of all health protection agencies in addressing the MBT-latex-rubber contamination problem:

Vaccines Containing Latex (Canada, August 2010)

Product Description	Trade Name	Latex site
Anthrax	Biothrax (BioSolutions)	in vial
Diph. Tet.Pertussis	Infanrix (GlaxoSmithKline)	in syringe

	Daptacel (Sanofi Pasteur)	in vial
	Tripedia (Sanofi Pasteur)	in vial
	Pediarix (GlaxoSmithKline)	in syringe
Hemophilus Pertussis	Hiberix (GlaxoSmithKline)	in syringe
	PedvaxHIB (Merck)	in vial
	ActHIB (SanofiPasteur)	in diluent vial
Hepatitis A	Havrix (GlaxoSmithKline)	in syringe
	Vaqta (Merck)	in vial and syringe
Hepatitis B	Engerix (SmithKlineFrench)	in syringe
	Recombivax (Merck)	in vial
HPV	Cerverix (GlaxoSmithKline)	in syringe
Influenza	Fluarix (GlaxiSmithKline)	in syringe
	Fluvirin (Novartis)	in syringe
	Fluzone (Sanofi Pasteur)	in syringe
	Agriflu (Novartis)	in syringe
Didh, pert. Polio	Kinrix (GlaxoSmithKline)	in syringe
Meningococcus	Menomune (Sanofi Pasteur)	in vial
	Menactra (Sanofi Pasteur)	in vial

Pneumococcus	Prevnar (Wyeth Lederle)	in syringes prior to lot D46873, not in lots D46873 and after
Polio	IPOL (Sanofi Pasteur)	in syringe
Tetanus diphtheria	Td (Generic)	in syringe
Tetanus diphtheria pertussis	Boostrix (GlaxoSmithKline)	in syringe
Yellow fever	YF-vax (Sanofi Pasteur)	in vial

Note that eight of these are for routine vaccination of children.

Note that the title of this document suggests that latex is the only contaminant to be considered in natural rubber. Whenever latex is a component of rubber, MBT is used as a catalyst during manufacture, and in my experience on two occasions of clustered allergic reactions, MBT was the dominant allergen being leached into injections. All natural rubber components of syringes and ampoules were made using latex, but clusters of allergic reactions were associated only with the presence of MBT as a contaminant of injections. This points to MBT as the dominant allergenic contaminant. Yet the serious reactions and deaths continue invariably to be attributed to an allergy to the childhood immunization vaccine, to the local anesthetic, to the antibiotic, or to the insulin, etc. Latex may be mentioned, but MBT has seemed to be forbidden territory, for some unknown reason.

During my two-year internship in internal medicine, I can remember my mentor, Dr. F.S. Brien, commenting that patients had experienced anaphylaxis from almost any injection — even from distilled water, which is devoid of any allergens. What these patients, their doctors, their dentists, and their nurses didn't realize was that in 1981, every time an injection was administered there was a high probability that they were being exposed to a significant concentration of MBT.

To a significant extent, government health protection agencies were then — and are still — allowing this known risk to persist, seemingly ignoring the possibility of serious reactions and deaths. Even in the hospitals that were believed to be natural rubber-free (latex-free hospitals), doctors and nurses were unknowingly injecting unsuspecting patients with MBT and latex.

Eight

Control of Medical Journal Content: Suppressing the MBT Contamination Warning

Much has been written in the last few years about the control that powerful pharmaceutical companies exert on the medical profession and its journals. Frequently it has been said that the largest lobby group in Washington D.C. is the pharmaceutical industry. It is believed that there are more lobbyists representing it than there are members of Congress.[1] This type of infiltration of Washington would not occur if it didn't result in legislation that benefited the industry.

This kind of influence has spread to infiltrate our medical journals. In 1999, there was an impression that the Massachusetts Medical Society had placed the reputation of its prestigious journal, the *New England Journal of Medicine (NEJ)*, at risk when it seemed to succumb to changing its direction from a not-for-profit journal to one that was profit-driven, with drug company advertising representing a significant component of the operating costs. A profit motive could render the *NEJ* more vulnerable to the interests of the pharmaceutical industry than most medical journals already appeared to be.

In 1999, the journal created new specialty journals under the logo of the *New England Journal*. This manoeuvre is said to have increased the profits of the NEJ from $386,540 per year (known profit in 1979) to an estimate of $20,000,000 for the year 2000.[2] The editor at this time, Dr. J.P. Kassirer, decided that he did not want his name associated with a practice he felt would jeopardize the journal's and his own ethical standards, by becoming vulnerable to lucrative forces with vested interests in promoting the use of pharmaceuticals. In a move that was generally considered to be a result of this ethical stand, Dr. Kassirer lost his position in 1999.

On February 20, 2006, John Hoey, the decade-long editor of the *Canadian Medical Association Journal (CMAJ)* was fired, as he said, because of "the censoring by the CMA of a report describing the difficulties Canadian women had in obtaining a Plan B (a nonprescription generic) drug from pharmacists."[3] Deputy editor Stephen Choi was named acting editor-in-chief, but when the CMA refused to adopt ten principles of editorial independence, Dr. Choi resigned, as did the editorial fellow and two associate editors.

Dr. J.P. Kassirer, now Editor Emeritus of the *New England Journal of Medicine*, and others writing in the *CMAJ*, the journal they were criticizing, cited the actions of the *CMAJ*'s owners and managers as "raising serious concern about the integrity of the journal, its reputation, and its viability in the community of top medical journals."[4]

It is worth noting that members of the Canadian Medical Association should take great care not to allow their journal to come under the control of any pharmaceutical corporation, because that should be recognized as being detrimental to the judicious practice of therapeutic medicine. Journals, especially our *Canadian Medical Association Journal*, are expected to exemplify the highest medical ethics.

It seems apparent that the editors of the *New England Journal* were expected to keep functioning strings attached, or they would be cut loose (fired, in these cases) by the medical societies operating the journals. Is it right for the journals' owners to allow their advertisers to manipulate the strings that govern the actions of the editorial staff, and thus dictate the contents of journal articles whenever they see fit? By sacrificing independence, a journal would be forfeiting relevance as a scientific source of medicine. Would journals thus become more like advertisers for pharmaceutical products?

On July 10, 2010,[5] and on July 13, 2010,[6] Gardiner Harris of the *New York Times* wrote that a major clinical trial (the "Record Study") of a popular anti-diabetes drug, Avandia (manufactured by GlaxoSmithKline) received "a scathing review." This trial, which was used by GSK to argue that the drug was safe, was examined by Dr. Thomas Marciniak of the Food and Drug Administration (FDA), finding "a dozen instances in which patients appeared to suffer serious heart problems that were not counted in the drug's tally of adverse events," something that "should not be found as single occurrences" in such studies. Dr. Marciniak said that, when interpreted correctly, instead of supporting Avandia's safety, "the study supports critics' contentions that Avandia may cause heart attacks and strokes."

Although the FDA had originally endorsed the Record Study in 2007, it was only after independent researchers, reviewing thousands of clinical cases, found Avandia to be associated with many dangerous side effects, that Dr. Marciniak undertook an examination of the cases studied in the Record — a multinational study of 4,447 patients in 23 countries, with type 2 diabetes — a study that was funded by GlaxoSmithKline, the manufacturer of Avandia.

In 2010, the *New England Journal* accused GSK of interfering with the trial's results,[7] while Dr. Jerome Kassirer, the former editor of the *NEJ*, raised the legitimate question of "whether the entire system is corrupt."

In 1999, a secret study on Avandia by GSK compared it to Actos, manufactured by Takeda. This study indicated that not only was Avandia no better than Actos, but that there was definite evidence that Avandia showed increased cardiovascular risks. Internal documents have proven that Avandia's manufacturer "spent the next 11 years trying to cover up" its own trial results.

A study of 227,571 Medicare patients, conducted by an FDA reviewer,[8] concluded that "Avandia increased the risks of stroke, heart disease, and death."

I direct the members of the Ontario Medical Association to another example of control of content of a medical journal by corporate interests. This came from personal experience. Because of my publications on allergic reactions associated with contamination of X-ray dye injections and the fastidious reporting of reactions to the Ontario Medical Association's Adverse Drug Reporting Program, I was asked to write an article for the OMA's journal, the *Ontario Medical Review*, on the contamination of pharmaceuticals by MBT leaching from the pharmaceutical rubber of syringes and ampoule seals.

Because the journal took great pride in its involvement in the reporting of adverse reactions to drug administration by OMA members, there always was a section devoted to the OMA's Adverse Drug Reporting Program. Our OMA journal had been dedicated to keeping Ontario physicians alerted to the importance of these adverse drug reactions, so this requested article should have been an informative one about the possibility of severe adverse reactions from MBT — an entirely appropriate article for the journal.

The article was carefully written and referenced fully, detailing my experiences with the two anaphylactic reactions to an injected X-ray dye contaminated by MBT. It was pointed out that this was just a glimpse of the MBT contamination that must have been occurring with injections of pharmaceuticals, IV solutions, immunization desensitizing "shots," and blood transfusions everywhere in the world. The final editing changes were made and accepted by the editorial staff. It was now in the form that would appear in print within a couple of weeks, warning of the potential for severe adverse reactions, an integral component of this journal's format and its *raison d'être*.

There should have been an aura of anticipation and pride among the offices of the *Ontario Medical Review*, as they were about to publish the world's third report on the topic. The article was to warn physicians about anaphylaxis events that had been occurring for years, but with the many severe reactions and many deaths worldwide being invariably blamed on the injected pharmaceutical, rather than the insidious contaminant, MBT. This was a very significant article indeed!

I read the galley proofs and made the suggested editorial changes. Two days after the final changes were made and approved, I was dumbfounded to receive a call from the editor, Dr. David Fletcher, who said that the journal could not publish the article because of the threat of being sued.

It must be said that Dr. Fletcher's reaction was the direct opposite of that of Tony Smith, the deputy editor of the *British Medical Journal* in the early 1980s. In answer to a similar threat of a lawsuit by a major drug company (Eli Lilly), Dr. Smith had the fortitude and integrity to firmly say, "In that case we'll see you in court."[9] The drug being cited by the BMJ as a cause of severe liver damage, benoxaprofen, was banned in the U.K. soon after the article was published. In the U.S., because of this reported hepatotoxicity, benoxaprofen was withdrawn in the same year it was marketed, 1982.

After pursuing a discussion with the editor for a few minutes, I realized that an absolutely final decision had been made — the requested, edited, revised, and approved article would not be seen in print.

I brooded and boiled over this development for hours, over the years of labour I had put into pharmaceutical rubber research, over the work I had done on the paper, and over the almost impenetrable barrier that continued to be erected to conceal the MBT hazard. Almost all members of the medical, dental, and nursing professions, and the public were destined to be kept unaware of the potentially lethal MBT hazard — with a respected medical journal aiding and abetting what seems to be an imposed restriction of medical teaching

It is obvious that the only groups that could sustain damage if the article were to be published would be the syringe manufacturers, and particularly the pharmaceutical industry, which had millions of pharmaceutical doses, prepackaged in unit dose syringes across the world, and probably a billion or more pharmaceutical ampoules with natural rubber seals.

It was obvious also that no lawsuit would have been considered, even remotely, because a court case of this significance would have resulted in many newspaper articles that would have the effect that they so badly wanted to avoid — the revealing to the public of the hazard that pharmaceutical rubber had exposed them to, and was continuing to. One should not expect that the pharmaceutical industry would be willing to sacrifice the health and possibly the very lives of patients for the sake of profits.

I had an uneasy feeling that the word "lucre" lingered somewhere not very far offstage, just hanging in the air. Pharmaceutical advertising is very lucrative for medical journals.

There are other facets to the manipulation of journals, brought about by their great economic power. The tampering with medical journals — even to the extent of attempting to prevent the publication of factual articles that the pharmaceutical industry would not like to appear — is well-recognized in our "free enterprise" world, not just my personal experience.

In 2006, a Toronto researcher, Joel Lexchin, writing in the *British Medical Journal*,[10] documented several examples. Lexchin cited one notable instance of what appears to have been economic punishment. After the publication of an article that "critically examined the scientific accuracy of advertisements for drugs in ten leading medical journals,"[11] the journal, using similar statistics from four other comparable journals, calculated that it had lost 1 to 1.5 million dollars in drug company advertising revenue from what seems to have been a punitive economic form of retaliation.

In the interest of medical ethics, one wonders if the pharmaceutical and medical rubber manufacturers could, or should, be alerted to the contents of medical journals before their publication, and then, inscrutably, almost cherry pick which articles get published (with reprints of these "vetted" articles being circulated to practicing physicians by pharmaceutical representatives as advertisements of their wares).

Nonetheless, the many millions (even billions) of pharmaceutical doses, insidiously in contact with natural rubber, were now destined to be used up on patients, with the attendant risks of severe adverse reactions that my patients had experienced, and the many deaths worldwide. The *Ontario Medical Review* apparently was aiding and abetting this unacceptable state of affairs by refusing to publish a pertinent article that they had requested I write.

One needs only to leaf through all medical journals to realize that almost all the advertising, and therefore, a significant percentage of the costs of the journals' publication, would be borne by advertising by the pharmaceutical industry.[12] This suggests that the real threat to the OMA's journal would not have been a lawsuit, but rather a stern warning that these manufacturers would withdraw their advertising if the MBT article were published. If this were the case, this would represent a glaring example of interference with the publication of an article that may have been detrimental to drug industry profits, but of great benefit to the interests of public health — the derailing of the dissemination of important information that warned of life-threatening MBT contamination.

It has been suggested, quite recently, that the practice of corporate power being exerted on journals, even to having articles "ghost written" by professional writers hired by the pharmaceutical industry,[13] may no longer exist. One questions, however, whether this behaviour has vanished, or ever will vanish, because it is so economically beneficial to the mutually interested parties. However, it is very degrading to the science of therapeutics in medicine and to the willing participants in this action.

Until even now this widespread MBT/rubber contamination problem has been largely buried — with hardly a headstone to disclose that it even existed. MBT was primarily written up in scientific journals that physicians almost never read, or refer to (e.g. the *Journal of Biomedical Mass Spectrometry*, or the *Journal of Chromatography*). It is deeply disturbing that such an important and pervasive public health problem can be so hard to uncover and virtually impossible to expose in print — and thus it has been so hard to protect patients from.

Benzothiazoles have been used in rubber manufacturing since the 1920s. The Canadian Worker's Compensation Board has for many years recognized MBT as a significant contact allergen in workers in rubber manufacturing. However, what has been discussed here is not just exposure to MBT through skin contact, but exposure by the far more dangerous systemic (injection) route. To my dismay, to this day MBT remains as a widespread hazard, virtually unknown to the medical profession, perhaps intentionally kept that way, with the active acquiescence of our health protection agencies, clinical scientists — and our medical journals.

Just as the MBT experience may be interpreted as a window to a far greater problem suggesting manufacturers ignoring, and perhaps actively suppressing, vital medical information, the recent travails of Dr. Nancy Olivieri, a world-recognized hematologist, may be seen to display a similar theme of improper corporate control. When a researcher reveals the adverse effects of treatments with a drug produced by a major manufacturer, the writer may find his or her position — and even a university appointment — at risk.

While receiving funding from the large pharmaceutical manufacturer, Apotex, for a drug trial on deferiprone, a treatment for a severe congenital anemia, Dr. Olivieri found that it may lose its efficacy with prolonged use. After consulting the hospital's research ethics board, she followed their advice and revised the consent forms for the patients enrolled in the drug trial, to inform them of this fact. (This had the potential to damage the marketability of deferiprone.)

Apotex forthwith not only terminated the two trials that Dr. Olivieri had in progress in Toronto, but they simultaneously terminated her consulting contract for a third international trial. Seemingly, Dr. Olivieri's scientific honesty had no place in the workings of this particular pharmaceutical corporation.

Some time after the trials were terminated, she found that there were instances of increased liver damage, with fibrosis, associated with this drug, above and beyond the liver damage from the increased iron storage that developed during therapy for her congenital anemia (thalassemia major) patients. This should not have been entirely unexpected, since congenital iron storage disease (hemochromatosis) is known to cause liver damage — and damage to the heart ("iron heart") and to the pancreas, with increased skin pigmentation ("bronzed diabetes"). In keeping with normal ethical standards,[14] she informed all of her patients and drug regulatory bodies of this risk.[15,16]

During this time, negotiations were underway with Apotex for the largest corporate donation ever given to the University of Toronto and its affiliated hospitals. Apparently, Apotex persuaded the U of T's president to write to the Liberal prime minister and four Liberal cabinet ministers regarding proposed new drug patent regulations, stating that "Apotex advised us that the adverse effect of the new regulations would make it impossible for Apotex to make its commitment to us." The president asked these officials "to do what is necessary to avoid the serious negative consequences to our very important medical sciences initiative."[17] The president apologized later for this conduct.

Conforming to the behaviour of a true scientist, Dr. Olivieri published her clinical trial findings on deferiprone. This action was motivated by the justifiable Ciceroic ethical axiom that the welfare of patients takes precedence[18] over the interests of a corporate donor (Apotex) — and the donation's recipient (her employers, the Toronto Hospital for Sick Children and the University of Toronto).

This termination of ongoing clinical trials that may not have shown a marketable result and that revealed a risk of permanent liver damage lays bare a huge ethics problem and a grave concern about the validity of publishing trial results in a way that can create a large bias in favour of pharmaceutical products. In this way, it would be possible to undertake 10 similar trials in different settings, using different investigators, and refuse to publish nine of the ten that statistically show negative effects and/or no positive effects. They then can publish the only one that may show positive findings for the trial drug.

A popular adage describes three degrees of increasingly bad lies — lies, damned lies, and statistics. One can understand how the worst variety may be published in our best medical journals. The other variety of truly valid trial results (the other nine out of ten cited above) — with the rare exception of that of Dr. Olivieri's group — may not appear in the tables of contents of our major medical journals, and may spell the demise of the careers of fine scientists (and perhaps the journals themselves), if they do appear in print.

In an action generally perceived as a consequence of her reporting of these drug trials, Dr. Olivieri, an internationally renowned medical scientist, was fired from her job as head of the Hemoglobinopathy (congenital abnormalities in structure of the hemoglobin molecule that result in anemia) Disease Unit at the Toronto Hospital for Sick Children.

There was an overwhelming outpouring of disgust from members of the medical profession and of the university academic community when they learned of this unconscionable interference with scientific integrity in research and with academic freedom. This pressure resulted in the rehiring of Dr. Olivieri, not by the HSC, but by the University of Toronto. She was not allowed to regain her previous position, because the HSC had unceremoniously dissolved it. However, she was allowed to continue her research on congenital anemias.

In recognition of her ethical stand as a scientist and as a physician who was willing to put her career in jeopardy, the University of Winnipeg bestowed on Professor Nancy Olivieri an Honorary Doctor of Science in 2006, citing that she was "one of the preeminent crusaders for academic freedom in our times," a "defender of research integrity, academic freedom, and as a critic of the increasing corporatization of the universities."[19]

This type of interference with the revealing of the true results of drug trials demands that there be legislation enacted so that those involved be absolutely obligated to register all drug trials and to publish the results, good, bad, or indifferent, if not in a journal, then in a recognized and easily accessed Internet site dedicated to revealing drug trial results. These drugs must be identified by all the generally accepted terms as to the class of drugs they represent and the purposes of treatment, so that the results do not remain hidden from other researchers, the medical community involved, or the public, some of whom will be personally involved in the treatments being investigated. The government bodies supervising the enforcement of the regulations must be immune to commercial pressures, with severe punishment for failure to abide by these principles.

Researchers, academic physicians, the editors and reviewers of medical journals, and the pharmaceutical industry, in theory, should be complementary — independent forces that combine in the public interest of the prevention and treatment of disease processes, something that should be a symbiotic relationship — mutually beneficial. However, as far as the pharmaceutical industry and the medical profession and their journals are concerned, a very intimate relationship has developed that has been compared to "dancing with a porcupine," wherein it seems that the results of research — and its publishing — must fulfill, for the pharmaceutical industry, a "fundamental need to satisfy shareholders," a powerful force that "could, and at times does, conflict with a researcher's agenda to seek and unveil truth."[20]

It seems that corporate power has always been exerted on journals, even to the extent having articles "ghost written" by professional writers hired by the pharmaceutical industry. Although it was suggested that this behaviour has vanished, it has not, as pointed out in the *Montreal Gazette*, August 24, 2009.[21] It is unclear whether it will ever vanish, because it is so lucrative to the mutually interested parties — yet so detrimental to the ethics of medicine and, potentially, so damaging to public health around the world.

Two Dalhousie professors, Elaine Gibson (law) and Françoise Baylis (bioethics and philosophy), noted that two reviews were undertaken to study the circumstances surrounding Dr. Nancy Olivieri's firing, the Naimark Review (commissioned by the Hospital for Sick Children)[22] and the Thompson Report (commissioned by the Canadian Association of University Teachers).[23] As might be imagined, diametrically opposite assignments of blame surfaced — with the Naimark Review exonerating the hospital and the Thompson Report blaming the hospital. The Thompson Report discredited the Naimark Review as being "based on incomplete, incorrect, and false testimony."

With great insight, the Dalhousie writers suggested that one must read both reports and decide "which version of events is more thorough, credible, independent and just."[24] In the final paragraph of their article, they offer words of caution to the much sought-after potential dancing partners for the pharmaceutical industry (the researchers, the academic doctors, the journal editors, and their reviewers): before accepting a dance with a potential porcupine, "one needs a clear idea of the choreography. When the music is unappealing, or the risk of missteps considerable, it is best to announce that one's dance card is full." This is an onerous responsibility heaved on the shoulders of those rendered vulnerable in the face of inadequate, or insecure funding.

Nine

An Expensive New X-ray Dye, Shown by Statistics to Reduce Serious Side Effects

Up to the mid 1980s, the X-ray dyes used for IVPs, arteriography, and cardiac imaging studies were slightly irritating to the vessels into which they were injected, causing some burning pain for a short time after the injection into an artery or vein. It was also known that the injection of these X-ray dyes was associated with adverse reactions that varied from nausea and vomiting, to anaphylactic shock, and sometimes death. Very serious allergic reactions were known to occur about once in 1,000 injections, with one death in about 100,000 injections.[1] Naturally, when allergic reactions occurred with these injections, they were attributed to allergy to the dye being injected. These were believed to be chemically pure pharmaceuticals, with no one considering the possibility of their contamination, especially by allergenic and/or toxic material.

In the mid 1980s, a new variant of these dyes came on the market. The injection of these new dyes was characterized by fewer minor side effects (nausea and vomiting, and burning sensation in the injection site). This decrease in minor side effects was considered to be due to their lower osmolality (relative absence of the tendency of molecules to break up into ions). These new dyes were therefore termed nonionic dyes, while the older ones were called ionic dyes. The main deterrent to the routine use of non-ionics in radiology departments was the price; the non-ionics were six to ten times more expensive than the older ionic dyes.

Great pressure was brought to bear on the users of these X-ray dyes when the results of a very large Japanese series (337,647 patients nationwide) were published,[2] comparing adverse reactions to the older ionic dyes to the adverse reactions when the very expensive new non-ionics were employed for IVPs. At the time of the study (September 1, 1986 to June 30, 1988), the injections of non-ionics showed significantly fewer adverse reactions. Particularly important was the determination that there were significantly fewer severe life-threatening reactions associated with the injection of the newer nonionic dyes, although no deaths occurred with either variety of dye in this series.

Quite naturally, the manufacturer promoted the newer, expensive nonionic dyes, not only for IVPs but also for the ever-increasing numbers of arteriograms, X-ray dye heart studies, and CT scans being performed. Medical, legal, and, creatively, philosophical, and even theological pressures were being injected into the promotion formula for advocating the universal use of these expensive non-ionics,[3] with the implication that it would be unethical, and even sinful — contrary to religious teaching — to use the much less expensive and, apparently, the more dangerous ionic dyes.

It was implied (though never said) that it could be malpractice to use the less costly dyes, because of the results of the large Japanese comparative series. This large study was used as a tool in the marketing of nonionic dyes, and reprints of the article were dispersed freely to any radiologists who might contemplate using these X-ray dyes.

Most hospitals in Canada and the U.S. switched to the exclusive use of non-ionics at great cost to their radiology departments. This change added many millions of dollars to health care costs every year, while filling the coffers of the manufacturers of the very expensive non-ionic X-ray dyes.

However, there was a flaw in the statistical reasoning being used. This was not just a minor flaw. It was a large flaw. In truth, it was an enormous flaw. One extremely pertinent factor was operating, biasing the comparative X-ray dye study,[4] unknown to the Canadian health care system, and unknown to the health care systems in the U.S. and globally, unknown to those in Japan injecting the dyes — but the manufacturers should have been aware of it.

This very large study was not done in Canada. It was not done in the U.S. The country that may have been carefully selected for this seemingly defining study was Japan.[5]

In any statistical study used to investigate effects and their causes, true scientists take extreme precautions to make sure some unconsidered factor is not skewing their results, making their studies invalid.

Consider the following facts:

- The very large series that showed decreased severe allergic reactions to the costly nonionic dyes was carried out in Japan.
- Japanese disposable syringes, since 1985, were all made with non-MBT, non-latex, non-allergenic, and nontoxic synthetic rubber syringe plunger tips.
- The ampoules of the new expensive nonionic dyes were sealed with synthetic non-MBT, non-latex, non-allergenic, and nontoxic synthetic rubber.

- The inexpensive ionic dye ampoules were sealed with natural rubber requiring allergenic and toxic MBT, and allergenic latex in the manufacturing process.[6]
- The first of my two severe anaphylactic shock reactions was proven to be from allergenic/toxic MBT from disposable syringes containing natural rubber (that just happened to be associated with the injection of cheaper nonionic X-ray dye).
- The second case of anaphylactic shock was from MBT leached into the dye from MBT in dye ampoule seals (again, associated with a cheaper ionic dye).

In light of this information, one would not have to read this Japanese article to know what the results would show. One would predict exactly what the authors would find in their study from September 1, 1986 to June 30, 1989, which was as follows:

The injections of "nonionic contrast media (X-ray dyes) significantly reduce the frequency of severe and potentially life-threatening ADRs (adverse drug reactions) to contrast media at all levels of risk, and that use of these media represents the most effective means of increasing the safety of contrast media examinations."

———

Those who knew what we have learned about allergenic MBT contamination and the presence of allergenic latex in medical natural rubber would have written their conclusions somewhat differently:

The contamination from natural rubber of any X-ray dyes by MBT, or latex, significantly increases the frequency of severe and potentially life-threatening ADRs (adverse drug reactions) to these contaminated contrast media at all levels of risk and that the elimination of natural rubber contact (made with the allergens MBT and latex) represents the most effective (and by far the least expensive) means of increasing the safety of any injections (ionic and nonionic contrast media, in this case).

In Japan, the risk of exposure to allergenic MBT had been eliminated in the case of the expensive non-ionic dyes, whereas the risk of allergenic MBT (and latex) exposure remained prevalent in the ampoule seals of the much less expensive ionic component of this study, thus introducing a very large bias towards causing allergic reactions with the cheaper ionic dyes, reactions that would be due to MBT, or latex, not to allergy to the ionic dyes. It was in the midst of this study that I encountered anaphylaxis from MBT contamination from the rubber ampoule seals, following an injection of one of the much less expensive ionic dyes.

Again one must be reminded of a type of intentionally introduced bias that led to that often-quoted saying, usually applied to political statistics, that there are three graduated kinds of lies: lies, damned lies, and statistics. Those knowingly speaking or writing falsehoods are generally classified as liars. It is important to note that these words do not refer to the Japanese researchers involved in this study; they were unaware of the insidious MBT-latex-natural-rubber aspect to the adverse reactions being reported.

However, there may be major medical, legal, ethical, and religious implications at the root of this saying (and there may be significant repercussions to each of these, as can be gauged from the second-worst type of lie) that conceivably may be factored into this statistical equation, if such prior knowledge was used by the manufacturers in the testing parameters and then in the marketing the expensive nonionic dyes.

Thoughtful, health cost-conscious, well-read radiologists in Saskatoon came to a somewhat different conclusion than their more credulous counterparts.

Just as there were reduced adverse reactions to costly nonionic dyes in the Japanese series, an anticipated reduction in the incidence of reactions to X-ray dye injections was being noticed, not in Japan, but in Saskatchewan, at the Royal Victoria Hospital in Saskatoon. However, this drop in serious reactions was not associated with the newer expensive nonionic dyes, but a reduction clearly was evident in the incidence of allergic reactions when the much less expensive ionic dyes continued to be used. The Saskatoon radiologists had understood a significant underlying increased risk factor in the reactions encountered with X-ray dye injections, and they realized that it was no longer present with the less costly ionic dyes.

Since 1990, they had known that MBT-latex-natural-rubber was no longer present in the disposable syringes they used to inject the dyes, and the seals on the cheaper ionic dye ampoules no longer leached MBT or latex, because they too were MBT-free, just as occurred when the costly nonionic dyes were injected in Japan.

Professor C. Stuart Houston of Saskatoon is a giant of Canadian diagnostic radiology, a six-year editor of the *Journal of the Canadian Association of Radiologists*, the author of five books on medicine, the history of medicine, and Canadian Arctic history, and a world-recognized authority in ornithology. With sound medical, economic, and ethical reasons, the Department of Radiology of the Royal Victoria Hospital in Saskatoon did not succumb to the exclusive use of the expensive nonionic dyes, but continued to use ionic dyes.

On this subject, in December 1994, he wrote to me that he had recently attended the annual November national meeting of the Radiological Society of North America (whose journal is *Radiology*) in Chicago. Dr. Houston described a session on "Selective use of nonionic contrast material (X-ray dyes): opposing philosophies, economics and ethics." The speaker had said that the expensive nonionic dyes were preferable to ionics but, because of cost, most hospitals still used a high proportion of nonionics. "[The Mayo Clinic is still at 85 percent ionics.]"

These are excerpts from what Dr. Houston wrote to me about what he rose from the floor to say in Chicago at this annual national meeting.[7] He prefaced his remarks by saying that his diagnostic radiology department continued to use ionic dyes and that Gavin Hamilton in London, Ontario, was like "a voice in the wilderness," and then continued as follows:

> ...Gavin Hamilton single-handedly had forced the removal of MBT from syringes and rubber stoppers in Canada. Since then we have not had a single serious IV contrast reaction at our hospital. Formerly, we had deaths, and we had serious reactions
>
> From the response, I suspect that no one in the audience had heard of MBT.

In the final paragraph of Dr. Houston's letter, in words that are etched in my memory, he wrote: "Please note in your memoirs that Stuart Houston is the second voice in the wilderness." In truth, this book represents a portion of my memoirs, comprising two significant areas of unfinished business in my life work, conjoined into a twin tale, as the reader is learning.

Although in 1994 natural rubber definitely had been removed from X-ray dye ampoules and from the syringes radiologists used to inject them, Dr. Houston's justifiable belief (and my hope), that natural rubber had been removed from contact with all drugs that are injected subcutaneously and intramuscularly, was not based on reality. There was, in fact, a failure to act on the acknowledged clinical concept that, although the intravenous route can elicit the most rapid onset of a deadly allergic reaction, any other means of tissue injection is far more dangerous than the ingestion of an allergen, but even the less dangerous ingestion route can kill, as those with peanut or seafood allergy have been warned repeatedly.

Dr. Elliott Lasser, an internationally recognized authority on contrast media, tapped into the FDA's database to compare reported reactions to ionic and nonionic X-ray dyes from 1990 to 1994.[8] Perhaps someone in Dr. Lasser's group was stimulated by Dr. Houston's 1994 comment about the reduction in the incidence of severe reactions when the cheaper ionic dyes were used. Dr. Houston had advised U.S. radiologists at their Chicago national meeting that this was a period during which there had been the almost complete elimination of exposure of X-ray dyes to direct contact with natural rubber, involving both ionic and nonionic varieties.

Lasser's group showed total reported reactions per million cases of 193.8 for ionics, compared to 142.5 for nonionics, a very close relationship, much closer than earlier studies had shown, when the incidence of natural rubber contact was far more common with ionic than nonionic dyes. What is even more important is that Lasser's group showed the incidence of fatal reactions, though low, was almost twice as high when the newer, much more expensive nonionic dyes were used (6.4 per million for nonionics and 3.9 per million for the older, much less costly ionic dyes).

The Saskatoon radiologists' experience and Lasser's study form an extremely significant validation of the extent of allergic reactions and deaths from MBT contamination of injections from pharmaceutical rubber. The older, much less expensive ionic radiopaque dyes have a long history of causing severe reactions uncommonly — and deaths fairly rarely. However, although the chemical composition of the dyes remained the same in 1990–1992, the incidence of severe reactions and deaths dropped remarkably when natural rubber contact was eliminated from the ampoule seals and from the syringes used to inject the MBT leaching from MBT-latex-rubber. MBT caused many deaths worldwide and remains a threat in Canada and the U.S., but the threat is extreme in India, China, and Indonesia, where MBT-latex-rubber is in common use in syringes, pharmaceutical ampoules, and IV apparatus.

This study destroys the safety issue as a major factor in selecting nonionic over ionic dyes. The decreased overall incidence in adverse reactions was not due to the "effect of improved contrast media," as this article suggests, but was due to the elimination of contact, of both dye types, with natural rubber and its leachates MBT and latex from syringes and ampoule seals. Dr. Houston's outstanding group of Saskatoon radiologists were not only Western trail blazers in this regard, but were showing the path the world should have followed in the past and must surely follow now in the rational future use of these dyes!

We are left to wonder what motivated the pharmaceutical industry to choose Japan for the huge study on IVP X-ray dyes, which led to decisions that have cost our health delivery system so much over the last 15 years.

Ten

Misdirected Protection of Government Health Protection Agencies, Allowing the Health Hazard of MBT to Extend Beyond 2000

In 1990, Dr. Ed Napke reviewed a book for the *CMAJ*, *Formulation Factors in Adverse Reactions* (A.T. Florence, 1990).[1] He commented that it was a "must read" book for those interested in drug reactions, but, in his review, Dr. Napke gave one severe criticism, as follows:

> One topic that is not mentioned (let alone emphasized) is the "leaching" from drug delivery systems. For example, 2-mercaptobenzothiazole (2-MBT) leaches readily from rubber and rubber-like products and can cause respiratory or cardiac arrest.

Also in 1990, I advised *Lancet* readers worldwide to "ask government regulatory bodies and manufacturers when natural rubber manufactured with MBT was last used in unit dose syringes and what are the expiry dates of the drugs involved."[2] To my deep dismay, one could ask that same question again, even in 2011, and still would find immunization vaccines, some insulin unit dose syringes, and some unexpired local anesthetics with their plunger seals made from MBT-latex natural rubber, and still eliciting allergic reactions and deaths.[3]

On August 31, 1998, the FDA's Health and Human Services issued a "Final Rule" for labeling. This rule, as applied to medical devices, was about clear labeling admitting when natural rubber is present. This "Final Rule" showing that syringe plungers, parenteral drug vial stoppers, and intravenous injection ports are included in the natural rubber exposure proves that they still existed on the market on September 30, 1998, when this rule came into effect.[4] For some inexplicable reason, in the Final Rule document, "the Center for Drug Evaluation and Research (CDER) and the Center for Biologics Evaluation and Research (CBER) of the FDA, which have jurisdiction over medication-device combination products such as pre-filled syringes, did not adopt the natural rubber latex labeling rule" and thus did not demand the removal from the marketplace of injectable pharmaceuticals that are packaged in unit-dose syringes in contact with MBT-latex-natural-rubber.

Thus, the rule largely remained a requirement focused on dipped rubber products, which have been shown to contain higher levels of releasable allergenic proteins than the dry, molded, natural rubber used in the packaging of medical devices. In spite of its dire warnings, this document contains the following perplexing non-committal statement: "... questions have remained as to whether the dry natural rubber used in pharmaceutical vial closures or plungers in syringes releases allergenic proteins, thereby creating an allergen exposure risk for latex-allergic individuals who receive parenteral medications."[5]

I felt frustrated at a state of affairs that seemed in defiance of basic principles of logic and public health — principles that should be the foundations of the U.S. Health and Human Services. The "Final Rule" was formulated, "in response to numerous reports of severe allergic reactions and deaths related to a wide range of medical devices containing natural rubber"[6] and still does not protect American citizens. Again, there was no mention of MBT. I cannot help but wonder whether the omission was intentional.

The admission by the pharmaceutical giant, Eli Lilly Co., in response to an inquiry after a patient developed a severe allergic reaction to an insulin injection, that: "the septum in the insulin vial was made from natural rubber,"[7] clearly showed that the natural MBT-latex medical rubber hazard was allowed to continue beyond 2000.

Headline News of a Life-Threatening Reaction to a Unit-Dose Syringe Injection

Those living in Alberta may remember the front-page colour photograph of a lovely woman's face under the *Globe and Mail*'s February 2, 2000, headline "Alberta NDP leader quits after near-death experience."[8] Had Pam Barrett not been an attractive woman, and had she not been the NDP leader, the article would not have been considered front-page material. However, such near-death experiences, and actual deaths, had been occurring repeatedly across the world. The majority of these would have been preventable if, appropriately, there had been the removal from the market of natural rubber products that were allowed to come in contact with injectable pharmaceuticals, including, in Pam Barrett's case, a dentist's local anesthetic, in a unit-dose syringe ("cartridge") probably with an MBT-latex-natural-rubber plunger part. I wrote to Ms. Barrett with this suggestion, but I believe, like all others who have suffered similar allergic reactions to MBT, or latex in injected pharmaceuticals, other reasons were given to her for the reaction (e.g. allergy to the local anesthetic injected).

Although Ms. Barrett died of cancer in 2008, she, her dentist, and her physicians would have been interested to know that, in 1990, two professors of pharmacology in Marseilles, France, who have written more on MBT contamination from pharmaceutical rubber than any other researchers, described finding MBT contamination in 28 local anesthetics dispensed in unit-dose syringes (the usual source of dental anesthesia) from five different manufacturers.[9] Such pharmaceuticals may have a shelf life of three years from manufacture, and were still being manufactured at the time of writing. This covers the time of Ms. Barrett's anaphylactic shock reaction to a dental local anaesthetic.

Government Health Protection: No Ciceros to Speak For Us

I am left wondering just whose health is of most concern to Health Canada — and in the U.S., whose interests are being served by Health and Human Services. The nearly inert behaviour of government health authorities, as exemplified in the information being presented here, is difficult to believe and impossible to justify, even generating despair at any future improvement in attitudes.

Cicero uttered an imperative proclamation to the legislators of the day, from the floor of the Senate, that is as apt today as it was in 51 B.C.E.: "*Salus populi suprema lex esto*" (the health and welfare of the people reign supreme).[10]

We could have used a Cicero in 1981, when the National Center for Drug Analysis revealed that MBT contaminated 50 percent of disposable syringe contents, and we could have used him again in 1983 when MBT was a proven cause of life-threatening anaphylaxis in London, Ontario, and we could have used him again in 1987, when it caused another anaphylactic shock in London. However, the Ciceros were ignored, silent, or silenced, since exposure to the hazards of MBT contamination of injectable pharmaceuticals has been allowed to persist, and the MBT hazard has been maintained as virtually unmentionable, into the 21st century.

As has been a characteristic of MBT contamination from the time of Reepmeyer's experience with it in 1981, the many potential Ciceros have remained silent, or largely unheard, perhaps even at times gagged (as in the case of the initial article written for *Radiology* at the request of a senior editor, and the requested and accepted MBT article in the *Ontario Medical Review*, which was finally rejected because of threats by concerned companies). All this is in defiance of the FDA's alarming words in 1998, when it admitted the significance of MBT-latex natural rubber allergens: the "Final Rule" was formulated "in response to numerous reports of severe allergic reactions and deaths related to a wide range of medical devices containing natural rubber."[11]

This natural rubber problem associated with injections that the FDA wrote about in 1998 was markedly worse in 1981 — but, in my own experience, it was still a hazard in 1987, by which time it should have been eliminated, and it remained a risk in 1990, when *Lancet* readers worldwide were warned that it might still exist.[12]

The Health Minister Questioned About the Ongoing Hazard of Pharmaceutical Rubber

My son, Dr. Kirk Hamilton, is a family physician in London, Ontario. Belatedly, I learned that in 2000 one of his patients suffered an anaphylactic shock reaction following the administration of a local anesthetic. This duplicated the life-threatening anaphylaxis experience mentioned earlier of the Alberta politician Pam Barrett, also in 2000. At the time, I had come to believe that natural rubber had been eliminated from all contact with injectable pharmaceuticals. Nonetheless, I decided to explore this through Health Canada.

On August 10, 2000, I wrote to Alan Rock, the Federal Minister of Health, asking him to answer "two principal questions for your ministry." These short, simple, specific questions were:

1. Is natural rubber being used in seals for local anesthetic ampoules, or for plunger seals for dental anesthetics?
2. If natural rubber is no longer being used, are there still some unexpired doses of such local anesthetics that are sealed with natural rubber (ampoules, or unit-dose syringes)?

    I am sure you will fully understand the gravity of these inquiries to which an early reply would be appreciated.

I had prefaced my questions by stating: "I have a research interest in the use of natural rubber as a sealing material for pharmaceutical ampoules and in the plungers of disposable syringes. My latest publication on this subject was in the *Lancet*, a copy of which is enclosed."

The "early reply" to my August 10, 2000, letter is dated January 23, 2001.[13] The Minister of Health, Alan Rock, in his very belated reply to my urgent request, reveals how the Health Ministry has failed to react to the dangers of products containing natural rubber that is in contact with pharmaceuticals meant for injection into patients, putting some in mortal peril. Important excerpts of his letter are as follows:

> The importation and sale of medical devices, including disposable syringes, is regulated by the Food and Drug Act and the Medical Devices Regulations. Disposable piston syringes are Class II medical devices pursuant to the

Classification Rules found in Schedule I of the Regulations. **Section 19 of the Act prohibits the sale of a device that, when used under customary conditions, may cause injury to the health of the purchaser or user thereof. Unfortunately, Health Canada cannot release information on the composition of specific syringe pistons and/or vial stoppers as this information is confidential**

Health Canada scientists are **monitoring** therapeutic product pre-market applications for natural rubber content.

The 2000 Compendium of Pharmaceutical Specialties also contains a **voluntary** list of Natural Rubber Latex free products.

Notice that there was no answer to either of my two simple questions, but it lays bare a policy that allows a few corporations to carry much more weight than the mass of our Canadian citizens. It seems that corporate lobbyists have managed to place their fingers on the scales — and to keep them there year after year. Furthermore, revealing whether natural rubber is present in syringes in no way infringes on manufacturers' patent rights. The confidentiality that the minister is protecting has resulted in hiding the exposure of Canadians to potentially lethal contamination of many of the injections by natural rubber leachates.

The faint echoes of Senator Cicero's 51 B.C.E. imperative directive to the legislators from the floor of the Senate still linger in the air: "*Salus populi suprema lex esto.*" The Minister of Health for Canada seemed not to hear or heed these echoes. This leaves Canadians exposed to MBT and latex allergens into the 21st century, in spite of Health Canada's own clear directive as cited in his letter to me: "Section 19 of the Act prohibits the sale of a device that, when used under customary conditions may cause injury to the health of the purchaser or user thereof." Perhaps it would have been helpful for the minister to discuss his ministry's position on this issue with Pam Barrett, who almost died as a result of such confidential contamination of injections by natural rubber allergens.

In 2001, the continued presence of natural rubber as a hazard was confirmed by a researcher interested in latex allergy, who, like most people, unaware of the presence of MBT and its implications, found two out of the five pharmaceutical vials tested had natural rubber seals, and reported the results in the journal, *Allergy and Clinical Immunology*.[14]

That local anesthetic unit-dose syringes ("cartridges") were still being made with MBT-latex-natural-rubber parts beyond 2000 is proven in a 2002 article by a group of Toronto dentists.[15] The authors write only about the possibility of latex allergy, remaining unaware of the coexistence of, and probably the even greater importance of the MBT allergy factor. Just as in Pam Barrett's near-fatal reaction, MBT or latex could have been responsible for many (if not most) similar anaphylactic reactions to local anesthetics and other injections across the world.[16]

An April 2003 U.S. Health and Human Services notice brings into question whether a privately run company should replace the division of the FDA, known as the Center for Devices and Radiological Health Office of Compliance, whose notice stated as follows:

Contains Non-binding Recommendations

Guidance for Industry
User Labeling for Devices that
Contain Natural Rubber (CFR

801.437); Small Entity Compliance
Guide for Industry

Document issued on: April 1, 2003

U.S. Department of Health and Human Services
Food and Drug Administration
Center for Devices and Radiological Health
Office of Compliance

The following are excerpts from this notice to
manufacturers;

- This *guidance* addresses specific federal regulations for
  labeling medical products that contain natural rubber.
- *FDA has noted an increase in deaths* reported to the
  agency that are associated with an apparent sensitivity
  to natural latex proteins contained in medical devices
- This document "describes the Agency's (FDA's) current
  thinking and *should be viewed only as regulations....*"
- The word *"should" means that something is suggested*
  or recommended, **not required**.
- 5) Representative examples of devices *that contain
  DNR (dry natural rubber)* include Anesthesia masks,
  electrode pads, *syringe plungers, parenteral drug vial
  stoppers, and intravenous injection ports.*

Notice that, yet again, there is no mention of the allergen
MBT — only latex.

There certainly was no Cicero around in 2005, when
a comprehensive 40-page document was compiled and
published in the *Journal of Allergy and Clinical Immunology*.
This article was "developed by the Joint Task Force on Practice
Parameters, representing the American Academy of Allergy,

Asthma and Immunology, the *American Journal of Allergy, Asthma and Immunology* and the Joint Council of Allergy, Asthma and Immunology. They jointly accepted responsibility for establishing "The diagnosis and management of anaphylaxis: an updated practice parameter," noting that, "This is a complete and comprehensive document at the current time." Thus, it was being promoted as representing the leading edge in defining the causes and appropriate treatment of the severe allergic reaction known as anaphylaxis (anaphylactic shock).

There are sections on:

- latex-induced anaphylaxis
- anaphylaxis during general anesthesia
- anaphylaxis and allergen immunotherapy vaccines

Although latex-induced anaphylaxis is discussed under three numbered headings, there is not a single reference to rubber contact with injectable fluids from disposable syringes, from ampoule seals, and IV fluid injection sets. The reader has learned now of the magnitude of the MBT/natural rubber problem and its nearly universal presence when injections were made using syringes with natural rubber components, by rubber components of intravenous fluid administration sets, and by rubber seals on pharmaceutical delivery systems. The prevalence of MBT in injected pharmaceuticals and fluids must have resulted in many instances of anaphylaxis worldwide since 1981. (Remember, there were two reports of anaphylaxis from a single private office, my diagnostic radiology office in London, Ontario, where only one pharmaceutical was being injected!)[17,18] By sheer coincidence, while neglecting to mention the rubber/MBT anaphylaxis risk, this "comprehensive" article cited my article relating the increased incidence of anaphylaxis in patients taking beta-blockers (beta adrenergic blocking agents).

We realize that there should have been a very large section devoted to the contamination of injections by MBT leached from medical rubber. To my dismay, there was no such section. There was not a paragraph. There was not even a sentence. In fact, there was not one single solitary word. Allergenic MBT was being allowed to remain unrecognized, unmentionable, made to lie dead and buried — without the enormous headstone it deserved.

Thus, in spite of the "numerous reports of severe allergic reactions and deaths," the document, in all its forty pages, chose not to mention natural rubber's potent allergen, MBT, in relation to the seals in pharmaceuticals for injection, and in unit-dose syringes. It did not mention even the possibility of anaphylaxis resulting from the contact of natural rubber win syringes, in ampoule seals, or in components of IV or blood transfusion sets — and this was supposed to be the leading edge in anaphylaxis. ("The Diagnosis and Management of Anaphylaxis: an Updated Practice Parameter.") Let the reader be the judge!

Failing to include syringe and ampoule seal MBT is certainly not an example of good medical practice. It is all the more disturbing because this document was produced by an assembly of many of the best allergists in North America, and it was meant to represent the leading edge in the understanding and treatment of life-threatening anaphylaxis. MTB was unmentioned, perhaps unmentionable.

A Summary of the Chronology of the MBT Allergenic/Toxic Problem

- 1969 — Guess and O'Leary studied the toxicology of MBT because it was being used widely as a vulcanization catalyst (accelerator) in rubber manufacturing, and natural rubber was being used increasingly where it was in contact with injections. In laboratory testing, they showed that MBT was toxic to animals and that it was a cumulative toxin with repeated exposures, while noting it was a known allergen. They pointed out that there was a particular risk to babies because the same size syringes were used to inject pharmaceuticals for babies and adults.

- 1981 — The FDA's National Center for Drug Analysis found that the false elevation of digoxin in unit dose syringes was due to contamination of the syringe contents with MBT, which was being measured as digoxin by HPLC (high performance liquid chromatography). Subsequent testing revealed that that MBT compounds leached into 50 percent of unit-dose pharmaceuticals from the natural rubber syringe plunger components, the same components used routinely and worldwide in disposable plastic syringes.

- 1981–1983 — In Hammersmith Hospital, London, U.K., Meek and Pettit found that MBT compounds reached "potentially toxic" blood concentrations in 91 babies, through repeated exposure to MBT compounds from natural rubber parts of disposable syringes, rubber seals on drug ampoules, and from natural rubber parts of IV apparatus and blood transfusion sets. This is a problem that must have existed in every hospital ward in the world in patients receiving repeated injections of pharmaceuticals, IV fluids, or transfusions.

- 1983 — A life-threatening anaphylaxis occurred in London, Ontario, from allergy to an X-ray dye contaminated by MBT leached from natural rubber in a disposable syringe. All injections in this office had used syringes with natural rubber seals, but it was only when significant MBT contamination arose that a cluster of increased reactions occurred, culminating in a life-threatening anaphylactic shock. MBT-free all-plastic Danish (Pharmaplast) syringes were substituted thereafter to eliminate MBT contamination from syringe rubber.

- 1987 — In spite of the exclusive use of MBT-free Danish syringes, another cluster of increased reactions, culminating in a life-threatening anaphylaxis, occurred in London, Ontario, from allergy to an X-ray dye contaminated by MBT from the natural rubber seal of the dye ampoule.

- 1990 — Katayama et al produced a series of over 300,000 patients undergoing IVP injections that showed a marked reduction in severe allergic reactions to a new expensive radio-opaque X-ray dye (non-ionic) compared to the older, much cheaper, ionic X-ray dyes.

- 1990 — Airaudo et al, out of 150 injection drugs tested, found 28 local anaesthetics, one epinephrine and eight insulin preparations in unit–dose syringes, and two Prednisolone acetate suspensions in rubber-sealed ampoules, were contaminated by leached MBT.[19]

- 1990 — *Lancet* readers were urged to confirm from the pharmaceutical industry that natural rubber, using MBT as a vulcanization catalyst, was no longer being used, or manufactured. They were informed that Japan had eliminated MBT rubber from syringes and pharmaceutical seals by 1985, and this could have caused the reduction in allergic reactions to the newer, much more expensive non-ionic X-ray dyes. The allergenic, toxic, embryo toxic, and mutagenic properties of MBT were discussed.

- 1994 — At the Radiological Society of North America annual national meeting, Dr. Stuart Houston rose from the floor to say that his radiology department in Saskatoon had experienced a dramatic reduction in serious reactions from the older, less expensive, X-ray dyes. The Saskatoon radiologists had continued to use the older non-ionic X-ray dyes in the belief that natural rubber contamination by MBT was responsible for most of their previous reactions.

- 1997 — Lasser et al, using FDA statistics from 1990 to 1992, confirmed the Saskatoon experience, showing that there had been a dramatic drop in the U.S. of incidence of allergic reactions to the less expensive ionic dyes, with the incidences in severe reactions to the use of ionic and non-ionic dyes being similar. However, although fatal reactions were rare with both dyes, twice as many died when the expensive dyes were used.

- 1998 — U.S. Health and Human Services issued the "Final Rule," condemning the use of natural rubber in syringes, IV apparatus, and other medical applications. This rule was formulated "in response to numerous reports of severe allergic reactions and deaths related to a wide range of medical devices containing natural rubber."[20] This rule was not enforced.

- 2000 — Hoffman described an attack of anaphylaxis in a child with diabetes Eli Lilly Co., in response to Hoffmann's inquiry about natural rubber in the unit dose syringes, admitted that: "the septum in the insulin vial was made from natural rubber." Physicians were unaware of the presence and allergenic significance of MBT leaching from natural rubber, and thus this particular allergic reaction was attributed to latex.

- 2005 — Johns Hopkins allergy and immunology researchers found pharmaceutical vial closures did not have to divulge natural rubber content, with 20 percent of vials sealed with MBT-latex-rubber.[21] They note that "pharmacists must contact the pharmaceutical company directly … to determine the composition of the closures."

- 2008 — Ten years after the "Final Rule," a July 2008 U.S. Government Centers for Disease Control document (updated August, 2010), "Latex in Vaccine Packaging," (updated August 2010) listed 29 vaccines with natural rubber seals in contact with the vaccine. GlaxoSmithKline manufactured 12 of these. Two of them were influenza vaccines (Fluarix and Fluvirin). From 2009 to 2010, there was mass vaccination of Canadians against the H1N1 influenza virus, with few serious reactions occurring — except in Manitoba — where one batch (170,000 doses) of the H1N1 vaccine, lot 7A, manufactured by GSK, was withdrawn from the market due to a significant incidence of severe reactions. All but 15,000 doses had been administered. In August, 2010, GSK admitted that their H1N1 vaccine packaging could contain natural rubber (MBT-latex-rubber). The clustering of reactions with lot 7A GSK H1N1 vaccine is suggestive of MBT contamination of the vaccine. My three months of badgering Health Canada has failed to get them to test GSK H1N1 vaccine, lot 7A, for MBT, using their own laboratories, which were installed at taxpayers' expense to perform exactly this type of public health-related examination. What is the function of our health protection agencies? Whom do they serve?

Through recent years, although the manufacturers and the governmental health protection agencies knew of the presence — and the deadly danger — of MBT-latex-rubber in their syringe plungers, an absurd distortion of truth was displayed in the description of some such natural-rubber-containing-syringes (including unit-dose syringes) as being "hypoallergenic" (not containing known allergenic material) — a terminology that the FDA told the manufactures in 2003 that they "probably" shouldn't use.

It has been noted that, in 2009, the B.C. Centre for Disease Control listed 28 immunization vaccines in unit dose syringes that had natural rubber seals. Of the 28, GSK manufactured three. It is suggested that the withdrawn batch of H1N1 vaccine associated with anaphylaxis and death may have been supplied in unit dose syringes with natural rubber seals, or that the batch may have been contaminated with MBT or latex from natural rubber contact prior to unit dose packaging, a previously recorded mode of MBT contamination of dental local anesthetics by Airaudo of Marseilles, France, the world authority on the subject.[22] Thus, the "mysterious poisoner" that was active across Canada in 1980–1981, alluded to by Professor Albert Burton in 1988 (concerning the HSC baby death epidemic)[23] may have struck again in 2009, this time in the province of Manitoba.

Information has been presented that appears to suggest the suppression of information about MBT contamination from health protection agencies, and interference with the publication of articles requested by journals on MBT contamination of injections.

Finally, although in Internet searches it is difficult to uncover the North American pharmaceuticals and dental local anesthetic cartridges that allow injectable pharmaceuticals to come in contact with natural rubber seals, it is far easier when searches are conducted regarding natural rubber products manufactured in India, China, and Indonesia, where this hazard continues to exist today on a very large scale.

Eleven

A Rubber Contaminant Linked to an Epidemic of Baby Poisoning in Toronto

In 1965, as a direct result of the thalidomide crisis that caused many severe limb deformities (markedly shortened arms and/or legs) of newborn babies and, following recommendations from the Royal College of Physicians and Surgeons of Canada, Dr. Ed Napke was called upon to set up a federal government adverse drug reaction reporting program, as a division of Health Canada. Dr. Napke designed a system of reporting that would signal when recognizable patterns were developing in these reported drug reactions, regionally or nationally. In 1968, when the World Health Organization started a similar international drug-monitoring program, the Collaborating Centre for International Drug Monitoring, Dr. Napke's expertise was recognized. With significant personal advice from Dr. Napke, the program came into being, Canada becoming one of the ten founding nations.

The fastidious reporting of all drug reactions encountered in my office probably was responsible for a disproportionate number of adverse reactions to X-ray dyes being filed with Ontario's branch of the Adverse Drug Reaction Reporting Program under the auspices of the Ontario Medical Association and overseen nationally by Dr. Napke. Many physicians, because of their large workloads, did not take the time to report many of their reactions, particularly the less severe ones.

In December 1987, Dr. Napke flew from Ottawa to London to see me. He was aware of the journal articles I had written on X-ray dye reactions and the significance of MBT contamination through medical devices and rubber ampoule seals, and realized that this contamination was being ignored.[1] He had been alerted to my dedication to reaction reporting through the OMA's Adverse Drug Reaction Reporting Program.

Also, I had recently written two case reports in the *Canadian Medical Association Journal* on the increased risk of anaphylaxis in the many patients taking "beta-blockers" (β-adrenergic blocking agents). This is a group of drugs that interferes with the action of the adrenal hormones, adrenaline, and noradrenaline that normally can raise the blood pressure and control the pulse rate. When two anaphylactic shock reactions occurred in my office in a two-month period and both patients were taking a beta-adrenergic blocking agent, it stimulated me to examine the interactions of the physiological activity of beta-blockers and the pathophysiology of anaphylaxis. My research suggested that, indeed, beta-blockers could amplify the blood-pressure-lowering effects of anaphylaxis, compounding this effect by interfering with the body's defense-mechanisms designed to counteract any drop in blood pressure.[2] It was, perhaps, the rebuttal to a severe letter of criticism of this relationship that attracted Dr. Napke's attention.[3] It was longer than the original article, with pertinent arguments about drug reactions and interactions.

Following these experiences with this class of drugs increasing the risk of anaphylaxis, my refusal to perform IVPs on patients taking beta-blockers angered some of my referring doctors. This was understandable, because in 1985 the international medical community did not recognize beta-blockers as being a factor in anaphylaxis. However, the increased risk of anaphylaxis in patients taking beta-blockers is currently accepted teaching by allergists, internists, radiologists, and urologists.[4,5,6,7]

The reason for Dr. Napke's trip to London was to determine if he could persuade me to oversee the OMA's Adverse Drug Reaction Reporting Program. This was a great personal honour, considering that Dr. F.S. Brien had held this post when he was my mentor during my two years as a resident in internal medicine. After a pause for thought, I thanked him, but saying that, although I would love to, it would be impossible for a diagnostic radiologist who was not involved in the active treatment of patients to achieve and to maintain the respect of the medical profession in this duty.

We sat for hours around the fireplace talking at length about what each of us had been doing. Then, after a long discussion about natural rubber contaminating pharmaceuticals, Dr. Napke, drawing on his years of scientific analysis of drug reaction reporting, looked up at the ceiling and floated a rhetorical question that was destined to influence my activities for years to come, even well into 2011: "Could your MBT contaminant have anything to do with the Toronto digoxin baby deaths?"

A gap in the conversation followed as I paused to reflect on the implications of this thought.

Then I said that probably it did not, because, in my experience, the life-threatening episodes in my patients were related to anaphylactic shock, and these severe allergic reactions were occurring at a frequency of about one per 1,000 patients, not at the frequency of deaths seen in the case of the Toronto babies. The HSC babies would not have had the years of multiple exposures to rubber allergens, as was the case in my adult patients who had many exposures to MBT over the years.

However, that night I woke up out of a deep sleep with the nagging thought that I had encountered digoxin somewhere in my research on rubber contaminants. I rolled over and fell back to sleep, resolved to go through my files the next day.

On leafing through my files, expectantly scanning for the word digoxin, I knew that I was going to find something significant. Finally the word flashed out of a page. I eventually found it in two places, one in 1969, in the article by Guess and O'Leary, and another in the 1983 article by Reepmeyer and Juhl.

Guess and O'Leary were studying the toxicology of MBT. They found that MBT was quite toxic to mice, with particular damage to the liver. Their further investigation showed that digoxin used alcohol as a solvent and that MBT was much more soluble in alcohol than in water, by far the most common solvent for pharmaceuticals. They noted that this finding might have particular significance in infant therapy.[8]

In the 1983 article from the U.S. National Center for Drug Analysis,[9] Reepmeyer and Juhl reported significant MBT contamination of drugs occurring with 50 percent of disposable syringes, coinciding with the time of the HSC baby deaths. The MBT leached from the natural rubber ends of the syringe plungers, with digoxin being one of the drugs into which leaching had occurred, in unit dose syringes. Like the 1969 findings of Guess and O'Leary, they noted that, because digoxin required alcohol as a solvent, and because MBT is 40 times as soluble in alcohol compared to water (the solvent used for most other pharmaceuticals), MBT contamination with digoxin would be greater than with most other drugs.

I was then thunderstruck by the bizarre coincidence that Yvonne Juhl had discovered that MBT could be measured as digoxin when tested by the HPLC (high performance liquid chromatography) test method!

Thus, MBT would interfere with the assay results for digoxin, giving falsely high digoxin readings when measurements were made using the HPLC method. This certainly could have been a factor in yielding the high digoxin levels in the HSC babies when the HPLC test method was being used.

Twelve

"There Were No Murders!"

I sensed that Dr. Napke's insightful question about MBT and the "digoxin" baby deaths had the potential to launch me into a long and difficult research project. I needed to know if there was any degree of uncertainty among members of the legal profession outside of Toronto about the theory of innocent babies being murdered by hospital staff nurses.

For many years, I had played a challenging weekly game of squash with Gordon Killeen, a highly respected judge whose legal knowledge and opinions were valued by his peers and whose decisions were just. He is a man with definite, carefully thought-out ideas, a man with great self-confidence, who would unflinchingly take a stand for what he believed in. Yes, this was the very person who could help me decide whether the Toronto baby deaths issue should be pursued.

In December 1987, I decided to confront him at a time when he least expected it, so that the answer would be unprepared and utterly candid. I knew he would have intently followed the proceedings of the Grange Inquiry, and would have been thoroughly aware of the behind-the-scenes legal and criminal developments from a site well removed from the actual stage on which this drama had been enacted. He would surely have formed an opinion.

The time and place chosen to confront Gordon Killeen were carefully selected, the shower room at the London Squash Racquets Club. We had just finished a vigorous, highly competitive, closely contested game and were towelling off when out of the blue, I fired the question: "Gordon, what do you think about the Susan Nelles/Grange Inquiry/Toronto Sick Kids baby deaths?" I phrased the question in this way exactly because I wanted to hit him with all the key elements of the case in one blast to get the maximum reaction.

To my amazement, what followed was far more dramatic and revealing than I could have possibly imagined. He froze and almost dropped his towel. His face turned white (with anger, I thought). Glaring right through me, transfixing me to the wall behind and, after a brief pause, he uttered two steely, staccato statements that were virtually spat from his lips and sent shivers up my spine: "There were no murders! It had something to do with digoxin."

The unsuspected linkage between two intertwined parallel contemporary chains of events had occurred. The structure of the many cross-linkages was now destined to be decoded.

The research, which was to continue for years, even to the present time, had just begun.

Part II

Incorrect Pathological Analysis in the Toronto Sick Kids "Digoxin" Baby Deaths

Thirteen

An Innocent Pediatric Cardiac Nurse is Charged with Multiple Patient Murders

It has been over 25 years since the Grange Inquiry Report (GIR) was released,[1] and over 29 years since, in a nightmarish chain of circumstances, Susan Nelles, a dedicated young nurse working in the Cardiology and Cardiovascular Unit of the Toronto Hospital for Sick Children (HSC), was charged with murder of infant cardiac patients. This would have been a devastating turn of events for any young professional, but particularly so for a nurse specializing in pediatric cardiac care and one whose father was a highly respected practicing pediatrician in Belleville, and whose brother was also a pediatrician.

The pathos in this tragedy escalated to a peak just before noon on March 25, 1981, when the young nurse opened her apartment door to a firm knock. Her small frame was dwarfed by the two large police officers, homicide detectives who were representatives of the Toronto Metropolitan Police, who filled the doorway. One officer said, "Are you Susan Marguerite Nelles?"

A visit by the police was not entirely unexpected, because she knew that others of the nursing staff had been subjected to questioning. Susan's roommate, Alison Woodbury, who was studying law at the University of Toronto, had cautioned her to refuse to answer any significant questions without having her lawyer present. Unfortunately, in a society where one is innocent until proven guilty, this refusal to answer questions would turn out to be tantamount to an admission of guilt in the eyes of the police, of the Crown Attorney's Office, and of the Attorney General.

After a period of intense questioning and after refusing to answer certain questions without her lawyer's presence, she was arrested on charges of the murder of four of her patients.

The two homicide detectives took Susan in a plain, unmarked police car, to be imprisoned in the court's female holding cell at the Metro Detention Centre. She withdrew into herself, stunned and silent, stranded in a precarious and vulnerable position, unprotected among some of society's most hardened criminals. Even such as they have their standards — and, many times in the past — such criminals had ways of meting out their own crude form of justice on one whom they felt was far worse than they were, a child murderer. Her person and her very life had been placed in extreme jeopardy.

Susan Nelles was fortunate to have enlisted the services of an excellent Toronto lawyer, Austin Cooper, to represent her at the preliminary hearing to determine whether she should be sent to trial on the four murder charges.

On his way to see this client he didn't know, Cooper reflected on the various motives that would incite someone to murder innocent and helpless children.

What kind of deranged creature could perform such cruel and callous acts?

Upon meeting her, he was struck by her small stature, the freshness in her face and demeanour, her politeness, and her appearance of normality. Her face had an aura of innocence and was reflected in her manner.[2]

He arranged for her release on $50,000 bail — after one week's incarceration — and prepared to represent her at the preliminary hearing.

Through wide experience gained in life and in the law, he had come to understand that one's own character is reflected in one's friends, Austin Cooper saw wholesomeness and integrity in all Susan's friends, among whom were her fellow nurses. He was most impressed by her best friend, her very supportive roommate, Alison Woodbury, a law student at the University of Toronto.

Judge David Vanek presided over this preliminary hearing into whether four charges of murder of cardiac ward babies at the HSC should be laid. The preliminary hearing would stretch on for forty-one days of testimony, with more than a hundred witnesses. The prosecutors, in cooperation with the Office of the Ontario Chief Coroner, laid out the evidence that they interpreted as pointing to murder, not just in four cases, but also in twenty additional babies.

Judge Vanek struggled through weeks of complex testimony from a legion of pathologists, physicians, pediatricians, biochemical scientists, and police investigators. It must be said that he had no training in medicine, no training in pathology and certainly no training in the biochemistry and in the pharmacology of digoxin.

Lawyer Austin Cooper prepared his evidence meticulously. His research into the hospital records showed that Janice Estrella had toxic digoxin blood levels on autopsy blood samples. He presented a chart showing the baby deaths and the nurses on duty at the time of death. This chart showed that Susan Nelles was not even on duty the night of Janice Estrella's death. Furthermore, the death occurred during a shift when the child was constantly attended by one of two nurses assigned to her case.

One piece of testimony that Cooper felt could be damaging to his case was evidence given to police investigators by Dr. Rodney Fowler, the acting chief of the cardiac ward during March, 1981. He related that, as he was leaving the ward after the death of Justin Cook, he glanced at Susan Nelles sitting at a desk in the nursing station, writing up the report on the death of her patient. He told police that he saw a strange expression on her face and that she showed no sign of grief after so terrible an event. The Crown Attorney would use this comment to strengthen his case for bringing Nelles to trial for murder.

When Cooper got Dr. Fowler on the stand, the doctor was subjected to a withering barrage of questions that would atomize any value his assessment of the expression on Susan Nelles's face might have had in this court of law. Cooper fired 55 short but deeply penetrating questions, revealing to Dr. Fowler — and to Judge Vanek — that one glance could not reveal the tearful, distraught sorrow that Nelles had displayed to others at the time of the death, but that had to be suppressed as she performed her duty in recording the terminal events on the chart of the deceased child, Justin Cook.

Ultimately, Judge Vanek factored in expert testimony that all the babies who died suffered from serious heart disease, were considered to be seriously ill, and that death in the near future would not be unexpected. He heard that, in the deaths later classified as murder, the attending physicians had concluded that, in every case, the deaths were from natural causes.

The generally accepted opinion of death from natural causes was overruled by the interpretations of findings, emanating from the pathology department's autopsy rooms, which slanted the thinking towards murder by intentional digoxin poisoning. These opinions did not originate from the attending physicians. They arose from interpretations of specimens taken in the autopsy rooms by a pathologist employed by the HSC.

Judge Vanek concluded, based on the testimony and the evidence as it was laid out before him, that there had been, indeed, four murders by intentional overdosage using the heart drug digoxin.

This hearing disturbed him greatly. Vanek's final decision came down to trying to balance all the testimony that the Crown prosecutors alleged pointed to murder against what he perceived as conflicting evidence. When he weighed in the innermost feelings that a judge may develop about whether a defendant is truly guilty, in his mind, the Scales of Justice tipped sufficiently to allow him to render his decision.

Vanek pronounced that the evidence presented "did not reach the threshold required to justify committal to trial." All four murder charges had to be dropped.

In the time that has elapsed since this hearing, it can be said now that it was his great insight and the very essence of the wisdom of Solomon contained in this statement, that made any future laying of murder charges against Susan Nelles that much more difficult.

Vanek stated much later, in his memoirs: "A defining moment, in my opinion, is an occasion when one is called upon to bring the full force of one's life experience in the solution of a difficult problem. My decision in the Nelles case was a defining moment in my career as a judge."[3] Although, for him, this was unquestionably true, to a far greater extent, it was a defining moment in the career, and in the life of an aspiring and dedicated young nurse.

Fourteen

Deaths by Insidious Poisoning, But No Murders

My involvement in the chronicle of the epidemic of suspicious baby deaths from July 1980 to April 1981 came about through Dr. Ed Napke's visionary statement in December 1987 about whether MBT contamination of injected drugs and fluids might somehow be related to these deaths. Dr. Napke's suggestion that MBT might be a factor harmonized with Judge Killeen's gut feeling and was expressed in his candidly emphatic statement about the HSC epidemic of baby deaths: "There were no murders."

———

Judge Killeen was fascinated that the evidence of the MBT contamination of pharmaceuticals emerged at the same time as the HSC baby deaths and that MBT toxicity, or allergenicity, might identify what, to him, was the unexplained cause of the baby deaths. I commented that these babies were all seriously ill, requiring many injections, and multiple exposures to MBT, rendering them more vulnerable to dying from repeated exposure to poisonous MBT compounds.

Unfortunately, my previous research had been focused, almost entirely, on MBT's allergenic properties that caused severe allergic reactions after a single MBT-contaminated injection. Not much thought had been directed towards the toxicity that could be brought on if MBT compounds reached significant concentrations with repeated exposures.[1] Allergic reactions required only trace amounts of MBT to exact a life-threatening cascade of consequences, just as a minute disturbance on a snowy hillside could trigger an avalanche.

Thus, MBT is a double menace — a two-headed dragon. The one head can kill quickly by a severe allergic reaction and anaphylactic shock. The other head can kill slowly, because MBT is a cumulative toxin that increases in concentration in the body with repeated contaminated injections.

The next week, before our game of squash, he handed me two government documents that I had never been exposed to before — the Dubin Report on the Hospital for Sick Children Review Committee, and the Royal Commission of Inquiry into Certain Deaths at the Hospital for Sick Children and Related Matters (the Grange Inquiry Report, or GIR). He had signed them out from the Library of the UWO Law School and said, knowingly, that it was unlikely that anyone would ask him to return these documents until he was finished with them. (I returned the documents within two weeks, having made photocopies of the pertinent pages.)

On reading through the material in the Dubin Report on the HSC, some of the passages brought tears to my eyes. When I encountered some of the evidence laid out in the Grange Inquiry Report, again the tears welled up as Judge Gordon Killeen's piercing words reverberated in my head: "There were no murders!"

As I delved through each document, when I read some of the details, I could not understand at all how so very much stress had been placed on some findings that had to be stretched to imply intentional poisoning by digoxin, while virtually no consideration was given to natural causes for the findings, and some obviously exonerating evidence was ignored completely.

I was disturbed greatly by how little attention was paid to the wild disparities in digoxin readings that clearly indicated there was something very wrong with the testing methods and with the interpretations of some of these autopsy specimen digoxin readings. Surely, the ignoring of potentially exonerating evidence should not be possible in such an important and extensive criminal investigation!

I developed a gnawing feeling that, somehow, emotions and suspicious thoughts were being allowed to suppress — disregard — and, worst of all — even discount, valid scientific and pathophysiological explanations for the findings. This resulted in the unjustified and, for Susan Nelles, the life-shattering conclusion that murder had been committed by an attending nurse. This disturbed feeling was destined to intensify gradually — until a final revelation of probable cause and effect seemed to materialize out of the shadows of the past, 30 years after the baby deaths.

Fifteen

The Dubin Report on the Toronto Hospital for Sick Children

The Toronto Hospital for Sick Children (HSC) is a world-class teaching hospital, legitimately recognized internationally for ground-breaking research and state-of-the-art medical and surgical treatment. Not the least of this involved the investigation and treatment of congenital heart disease. In spite of this excellence, in the period from July 1980 to April 1981, the HSC was experiencing an unusual and very disturbing increase in the number of baby deaths in the hospital's cardiac wards. Because of this great concern, Justice Dubin was called in to examine the workings of the hospital, to ascertain if there were any general areas where there might have been deficiencies and where improvements appeared to be warranted.

The Dubin Report on the Hospital for Sick Children Review Committee, released in January 1983, was purely fact-finding on the functioning of the hospital at the time of the increase in baby deaths. Justice Dubin was informed of a disturbing increase in the number of deaths occurring on the hospital's cardiac wards 4A and, especially, 4B. He noted: "Although all these patients were seriously ill and death in the near future was not completely unexpected, their deaths were not expected at that time."[1] However, based on interpretations of blood specimens taken in the autopsy room, a theory arose that the increase in deaths was due to poisoning by intentional digoxin over-dosage.

One must be aware that the sole reason for hospitals classifying patients as seriously ill is to prepare families for deaths that could occur at any time, regardless of the fact that the babies were receiving the best medical care possible, and that all of the babies who died were classified by the HSC attending staff as being in the category of "seriously ill."

Dubin's 236-page report questioned why it took so long for the HSC to act on what was obviously an increased death rate. He raised the very real issue of medication errors and suggested the more general use of unit dose syringes — precisely measured doses of pharmaceuticals, preloaded at the factory. He proposed that the general use of this method of medication administration would significantly reduce the chance of dosage errors. The reason his attention was drawn to this method of drug administration was at least partially due to the intensive promotion of this method of drug administration by the pharmaceutical companies. This accurate dose delivery system was significantly more expensive than the use of multi-dose ampoules.

However, as you will learn later, while guaranteeing exact dosages of drugs, these unit dose syringes had expiry dates of up to three years following manufacture. Throughout this time, the syringe contents would be in intimate contact with the components of the syringes, which would turn out to be unsuspected conveyors of chemical contaminants, particularly at the time of the HSC baby deaths.

Ted Bissland, a longtime CBC journalist and a specialist on legal affairs, related that at the time of the Dubin Inquiry, the medical staff at the HSC had appointed pediatrician Dr. Harry Bain to assess the deaths in question. Previously, Dr. Bain had been the Professor of Pediatrics for the University of Toronto Medical School and head of Pediatrics at the HSC. After intensive study of the hospital records, he formed the opinion that "all the patients had underlying conditions that could have caused cardiac arrest and death." However, he admitted that it was "possible that toxic levels of digoxin could also have been the cause."[2]

Sixteen

The Grange Inquiry Report

Justice Samuel Grange of the Ontario Court of Appeal was appointed by the Government of Ontario to head a "Royal Commission of Inquiry into Certain Deaths at the Hospital for Sick Children and Related Matters," under the Public Inquiries Act, which will be termed the Grange Inquiry Report, or the GIR. This was to be, essentially, a fact-finding inquiry into the increased number of deaths occurring on the cardiac wards in the period of July 1980 to April 1981.

When the inquiry began, it was inconceivable that it would take seventeen months to complete its work and that it would also consume many hours of national television coverage, day after day, week after week, and month after month. The overexposure of the viewers to multiple deaths and poisonings began to have a numbing effect.

The "Terms of Reference" for this inquiry prohibited Grange from assigning guilt, from naming, or from suggesting anyone he might consider responsible. Grange, apparently with a feeling that that kind of directive shouldn't apply to him, resisted such a restriction. While admitting knowledge of this prohibition, Grange nonetheless decided to note the "constant presence of one or more members of that team of nurses" at the various times of death. He also underlined the significance of this statement by admitting that this observation "might well be deemed at least a partial identification of the killer or killers." Note that in this fact-finding inquiry he announced absolutely that homicides had been committed, leaving no opening for death by natural causes, which, in every case, was the conclusion of the attending doctors — at least until conclusions started to be drawn from specimens taken in the autopsy rooms.

On page four of his report, Grange made a significantly revealing statement, almost as an aside, that: "Perhaps there will be some evidence which has influenced me in reaching my conclusions upon which I can neither report nor comment." This is a very strange statement for the commissioner to include in a Royal Commission of Inquiry Report. I have come to believe that Grange was indicating that the "evidence" that he referred to must not have been provable facts, but rather someone's analysis had impressed him immensely. I sensed that there was someone in the shadows feeding Grange allegations, biasing him towards belief in the multiple murder theory, a very persuasive someone whose name was not apparent to me in my research. I suspected all along that it was someone in the Office of the Ontario Chief Coroner, perhaps even the chief coroner himself. One has the right to expect a royal commissioner to be immune to such influence when it is not based on provable facts.

I believe that Grange's report intentionally left little doubt that an accusing finger was pointing directly at Susan Nelles as the perpetrator of the multiple murders.

When faced with the high digoxin readings on autopsy specimens, Grange called in the Toxicology Section of the Centre of Forensic Sciences (CFS) to confirm the readings. At the time of the HSC baby death investigation and the Grange Inquiry, it was under the aegis of the Office of the Attorney General of Ontario.

The Toronto Centre is among the largest and best forensic science facilities in North America, with a smaller centre serving Canada's north (Northern Regional Laboratory of Sault Ste. Marie). These laboratories do highly specialized forensic investigation involving biology, chemistry, document examination, electronics, firearms, and toxicology. It was the toxicology section that Justice Grange contacted to perform digoxin analyses.

In its role in criminal cases, its motto, "*scientia pro justicia*" (science for justice), indicated that it strove to provide purely scientific results — uninfluenced by the power of the police or the prosecutors for the Crown.

The CFS assigned Dr. George Cimbura, its head scientist, to perform the biochemical analyses required for this inquiry. Although Justice Grange relied heavily on the CFS digoxin testing results, both Dr. Cimbura and Grange acknowledged that the Centre had no previous experience in doing or interpreting digoxin tests. Grange's admission is quite relevant to the digoxin testing by the CFS, but it had a much greater significance in relation to the interpretation of these post mortem digoxin levels by the pathologists, biochemists, and the attending medical staff.

Although it was common practice for digoxin blood levels to be monitored in patients being treated with digoxin, post mortem digoxin specimens were undergoing analysis for the first time at the HSC, on specimens taken in the autopsy rooms, with far too much reliance being placed on the interpretation of these post mortem results. Furthermore, digoxin levels on exhumed bodies had never been done before, anywhere. Thus, there were no "normal" standards to use in comparison.

Dr. Peter Macklem, Professor of Medicine at McGill and a leading Canadian medical researcher, denounced drawing any conclusions at all from such post mortem samples.

Seventeen

The Digoxin Poisoning Investigation

The police have an essential role to play in the investigation of an alleged murder.

In my childhood, my parents taught respect for the police and, if ever I found myself in trouble, I was instructed not to be afraid to ask a police officer for help. They taught, correctly, that each day, whenever the police put on their uniforms, they might have to put their lives on the line to protect us and to maintain the law and order that is a characteristic quality of a civilized society.

At the time of the HSC baby death inquiry, the Toronto Metropolitan Police were informed that multiple murders had been committed and that a hospital nurse was probably responsible. This conclusion was based on circumstantial evidence and on interpretations of findings from autopsy rooms — apparently interpretations that were readily accepted by the Office of the Ontario Chief Coroner. However it was not until the very last baby death that Dr. Bennett, the Chief Coroner, came to believe he was dealing with a mass murderer.[1]

Once murder was decided upon, it now was the overriding duty of the police to tie these murders to the alleged perpetrator, alleged to be a nurse named Susan Nelles.

Interspersed with the weight of the circumstantial evidence being amassed against Nelles was some evidence that appeared to be exonerating. That evidence seemed to be brushed aside, not just by the police, but also by the pathologists, by the attending physicians, by the Office of the Ontario Chief Coroner, and by Grange. There seemed to be some driving force behind the murder theory, someone not mentioned at all in the GIR — someone behind the scenes, but apparently still capable of acting as the director of this tragedy of baby deaths — someone apparently acting out a role as an advocate for the Crown, seemingly in an attempt to perhaps even skew the evidence to prop up the case for mass murder.

While concentrating on criminal culpability, police should be permanently on high alert for exonerating evidence. It takes extreme vigilance at times not to allow prosecutors to render themselves blind to the point of contributing to innocent people being charged and even convicted. However, there can be circumstances, such as in this case, that extend beyond a police officer's expertise, in which false interpretations of highly technical evidence by those considered to be the experts can lead to false charges being laid.

There are examples in law of this kind of expert testimony. A case in point can be found in the October 1, 2008, findings of the Goudge Inquiry. Justice Goudge documented that in the decade 1991 to 2001, Dr. Charles Smith, playing the role of a pediatric forensic pathologist, through his engaging personality and his authoritative stance, was able to bias his opinions on evidence by crafting his interpretations of autopsy findings to suit a preconceived — and often erroneous opinion — that child murders had been committed. He was a very convincing witness. Belatedly recognized to everyone's extreme regret, this led, ultimately, to many false accusations of the murder of children, to convictions, and to many false imprisonments. Justice Goudge cited twenty cases in a ten-year period that definitely resulted in miscarriages of justice, with murder convictions based on Dr. Smith's incorrect interpretations of baby autopsy findings.

In the case of the HSC baby death epidemic, there were a number of pieces of evidence that might have alerted police, and certainly should have alerted physicians, particularly the Office of the Ontario Chief Coroner, that murders had not been committed.

Symptoms and Signs of Digoxin Toxicity

Initially, with each of the deaths later classified as murder by digoxin poisoning, as Grange commented: "Suspicion of toxicity as a cause of death was rarely if ever entertained simply because, as the Mortality and Morbidity Conferences amply demonstrated, the clinical condition of the child was thought, generally speaking, fully to explain the death."[2] One must realize that, in reaching the initial conclusion at these conferences that the deaths were from natural causes, the patients' clinical condition, course in hospital, and the circumstances at the time of death were discussed carefully. There was no thought of murder until a theory arose based on specimens taken by a pathologist working in the autopsy rooms.

As the theory of murder rather than natural causes of death gained momentum, much was made of the assumption that the babies were dying with signs and symptoms characteristic of digoxin intoxication — nausea and vomiting, various heart irregularities, electrolyte disturbances. It must be emphasized that these were nonspecific symptoms and signs, seen in many illnesses and conditions — for example, hepatitis of viral or toxic origin can cause nausea and vomiting. These symptoms and signs only became related to digoxin after what were interpreted as high digoxin readings came out of the blood samples taken by the pathology department from the autopsy rooms at the HSC, hours after death.

You can ask any mother what happens when her baby is upset from any cause, or gets a fever from any cause, or coughs, or eats something unpleasant. She would reply that, in many of these cases, her baby would likely vomit.

Every one of the children who died had come into the hospital emotionally upset. Each had been taken from home seriously ill from life-threatening congenital heart disease. The nature of the various types of heart disease and the different drugs used to treat them (e.g. digoxin, propranolol, atropine) can contribute in their own way to the various disturbances in heart rate and rhythm described as the babies became more seriously ill. Forcing any patient, particularly a child, to take any kind of medicine can induce vomiting. The vomiting, the diuretics, and known renal disease would contribute to disturbances in the blood chemistry.

However, the significance of these "natural" causes was overshadowed by a focus on digoxin toxicity as the only possible cause to be considered for these symptoms and signs. The diagnosis of digoxin toxicity, arising out of interpretations of post mortem autopsy digoxin readings, was allowed to supplant the original diagnoses of the attending physicians that had, in every case, been death from natural causes.

Contradictions to Digoxin Poisoning

The Grange Inquiry was meant to be only a fact-finding exercise, but with the added substantial power to subpoena witnesses. The witnesses' testimony could not be used against them in a court of law. It was not — and should not have been — part of Grange's mandate to assess guilt, or to impose penalties. That is why such a legal process is called an inquiry. That was what the Terms of Reference for the inquiry clearly stated, with the expectation that Justice Grange would abide by these rules.

However, in spite of these clearly defined limitations. Grange could not be diverted from suggesting what he had been led to believe — that Susan Nelles was a mass murderer. Scrutiny of some of the details in his report (that even a non-scientist should have recognized), and other information available at the time, or shortly thereafter, clearly indicated that there were no murders.

There was something drastically wrong with the digoxin testing and something even more wrong with extrapolating autopsy digoxin readings, to have the same significance as digoxin measurements in the circulating blood of a living patient.

Using the information available to everyone else at the Grange Inquiry, Dr. Peter Macklem, a world-renowned medical scientist, formed his own carefully thought-out opinion, that the increased death rate was likely from natural causes. Dr. Macklem defied the prevailing theory by making this statement (regarding post mortem digoxin measurements in babies): "The results of such measurements would have been useless" without comparing them with digoxin measurements on a control group of similar babies who had died of natural causes.

During the inquiry, so convinced was he of the lack of validity of some of the digoxin testing being done, that he "launched an unbridled attack" on Dr. George Cimbura's testing methods at the CFS, in a lecture to the Canadian Society for Clinical Investigation."[3] When Dr. Cimbura's lawyer informed Grange of this, Grange asked for an apology from Dr. Macklem.

Although Dr. Macklem offered the apology, he clarified that episode in the following way:[4]

It occurred towards the end of the day and I had
been on the stand since the morning and was
getting pretty tired. I immediately regretted my
apology and wished I had said something like,
"This is a scientific controversy. If one happens
to be right and the other person wrong, then
one must never apologize for getting closer to
the truth. That's the function of science and if
someone's reputation suffers as a result that's
also the way science works."

However, probably as a direct result of Dr. Macklem's
question about the lack of control studies, Dr. Cimbura, a
research scientist at the Centre of Forensic Sciences, undertook
such a scientific study. He analyzed digoxin levels on autopsies
performed on 14 children who died while taking digoxin (GIR,
page 110) to determine if, under these circumstances, high
digoxin readings could be found. One child's specimen in this
very small control group, taken at the time of the autopsy, showed
a postmortem digoxin reading of 169.6 ngms per mL. It must be
emphasized that 169.6 ngms per mL represents a reading 200
times the expected therapeutic blood level for digoxin — and a
level significantly higher than any others that were cited in the
GIR as evidence of murder by intentional digoxin poisoning.

How could any reasonable trained investigator ignore such
an astonishing result?

This proved, absolutely, the validity of Dr. Macklem's
insistence on the scientific use of a control study. Such a high
reading indicated the natural occurrence of extremely high
digoxin readings, possibly arising from the tests measuring
other substances in the blood specimen as digoxin.

One must emphasize that the digoxin reading in the case of
J.E., one of the alleged murder victims, that registered 72 ngm/
mL, caused such alarm among HSC medical technicians that

they repeated the testing six times on the same specimen.[5] Why was J.E.'s death classified as murder when the digoxin test reading was 72 ngms per mL, and why was a reading of 169 ngms per mL assigned to natural causes in Dr. Cimbura's control series? This control study was done for the sole purpose of determining if high readings were possible under normal circumstances, yet the results were ignored.

The great significance of this very high digoxin reading in a control study group was ignored by the pathologists, ignored by the medical staff, ignored by the Office of the Ontario Chief Coroner and, most importantly, ignored by Grange. Of this one fact you can be absolutely certain, this single piece of evidence, presented to a judge and jury by a good criminal lawyer, would have been used to completely destroy the theory of murder by digoxin poisoning. Common sense tells us there was something very wrong with the digoxin testing and with the interpretation of the readings on autopsy specimens at that time, the common sense that all judges must possess, and all jurors are expected to apply in their deliberations.

Some other undetermined factor caused the epidemic of increased baby deaths and some undetermined factor caused the very high digoxin readings. These readings distracted the investigators, preventing them from exploring any other causes to explain the increased death rate in the infant cardiac patients.

The Atlanta Centers for Disease Control

The baby death period represented a variant of an epidemic and was termed such by Grange. Dr. Harry Bain and other members of the HSC medical staff felt that it was reasonable to call in experts on the statistical analysis of epidemic patterns, a method that had been of proven worth in tracing the source of epidemics caused by disease organisms. To get an independent epidemiological study of the HSC baby death epidemic and to gather and analyze the data, the Atlanta Centers for Disease Control was brought in through a formal request by the Ontario Ministry of Health.

The ACDC epidemiologists looked at all the information that was available and which you are reading now, consulting with the pathologists, biochemists, and attending physicians, and then did a statistical study. In the end, the ACDC concluded that at least seven babies died from an overdose of digoxin in the 1980 to 1982 period and that there were an additional 21 babies who were suspected of digoxin poisoning.

Grange placed great significance on the ACDC's opinion.

As the reader now understands, there was clearly defined information that was available at the time of the GIR — and which was available to the ACDC — that showed digoxin toxicity to be unlikely as the cause of the increased death rate. With the respect gained by the ACDC over the years for competence in its epidemiological studies, one would believe that the conclusions should not be swayed unscientifically by any personality in the Office of the Ontario Chief Coroner. However, as it turned out, "The ACDC definitely ignored some glaring inconsistencies in the digoxin tests in this study, surely one of their least memorable ventures into epidemiology."[6] Only their tested scientific methods of analysis should have formed the foundations of the ultimate ACDC report!

Eighteen

Falsely High Digoxin Readings on the Autopsy Digoxin Tests

Until the time of the HSC baby deaths, the medical staff (pathologists, cardiologists, pediatricians, and cardiac surgeons) had little experience in taking or interpreting post mortem digoxin tests. They were being done for the first time during the baby death epidemic, yet the interpretations of these first-time-ever digoxin tests formed the basis for murder charges being brought against an innocent nurse.

In his report, Grange noted that a particular digoxin test done on J.E., on fluid taken by the pathologist from the abdominal cavity, in the HSC autopsy room (GIR, pages 107, 108) was "perhaps the first in the hospital's history." In truth, it wasn't "almost" the first. It was the very first — and the two different test specimens that were procured were very unusual indeed, unique in the history of digoxin specimen-taking, and yet the results were being construed as evidence of murder by digoxin poisoning.

Two J.E. samples were taken in the morgue for digoxin analysis in the HSC biochemistry laboratory, using the Beckman RIA (radio-immunoassay) test method. These specimens were obtained by the pathologist at least 15 hours after death (and even hours after the autopsy had been completed), one sample from a leg vein and another — not from venous blood as was usual — but from blood and bile-stained fluid in the pelvic portion of the abdominal cavity.

It should be remembered, particularly, that some of this fluid would be blood that had spilled out from the heart and great vessels as they were removed during the autopsy. This blood had been in contact with dead heart muscle cells for some hours after death. At the time, there were no standards anywhere in the world with which to compare the results, but the results of these tests would form the basis for stating that the high digoxin readings signified death from digoxin poisoning.

The digoxin reading from this first-time-abdominal-cavity-fluid would prove to be the highest of all the post mortem tests, but careful note must be taken that the digoxin reading was not nearly as high as one of Dr. Cimbura's similar "control series" reading, taken during the Grange Inquiry. As is now crystal clear, the crucial value of Dr, Cimbura's control study was both exonerating and completely ignored.

The RIA (radio-immunoassay) test and the HPLC (high performance liquid chromatography) were the only two methods of digoxin testing used in the HSC baby death investigation. The RIA method was the only test used by the HSC. The Centre of Forensic Sciences started out using only the RIA test method. It was not until "the late summer of 1981 that the HPLC test was also used."[1]

The RIA test was just one source of falsely high digoxin readings. Based on the evidence placed before him during the Inquiry, Grange noted about the RIA test: "The level recorded may thus include digoxin-like substances as well as digoxin and thus give a falsely high reading...."[2] The very high autopsy digoxin reading on J.E. was initially believed to be due to the presence of another substance which was improperly read by RIA as digoxin (digoxin-like immunoreactive substance, or DLIS), but this interpretation was soon discarded in favour of intentional digoxin poisoning.

A single autopsy blood sample from baby K.P. was divided into three test tubes. Each of these identical samples was tested by RIA in three different laboratories, the HSC, the Centre of Forensic Sciences, and Mount Sinai Hospital. The HSC and the Centre of Forensic Sciences reported digoxin readings of 26 ngm per mL. However, something that should have caused loud alarm bells to sound was that the RIA testing at Mount Sinai Hospital revealed an extremely high digoxin reading of 112 ngm per mL (GIR page 136). On the very same blood sample, using RIA testing, a discrepancy was found of more than 400 percent. Such a discrepancy would disqualify any blood digoxin levels measured by this method. The Mount Sinai RIA test was measuring some digoxin-like immunoreactive substance (DLIS) as digoxin at a very high level, 86 ngm per mL higher than the other tests. Remember the digoxin blood level should be around 1 ngm per mL!

Common sense dictates that a discrepancy of this magnitude should have nullified the significance of any other high readings using RIA tests. Imagine how this major information would be played out, in a court of law, in front of a judge and jury. From his wide experience in court as a judge, Grange should have been particularly aware of the relevance of this type of evidence when presented to a thoughtful judge and jury, but in this case, there was no jury — and the judge was Justice Grange — who was determined to write in his final report that there was a "killer or killers," seemingly a much harsher terminology than the usual legal description, "murderer, or murderers."

The extremely high Mt. Sinai RIA test result was a flagrant example showing the wild inaccuracy of all RIA tests in general use at the time. The Beckman RIA test, the only digoxin test method used by the HSC, was singled out by Dr. S.W. Graves, a Harvard medical specialist, as being "among the very worst" of these high reading inaccurate tests.[3] The Beckman test method was taken off the market shortly after the GIR because, as the manufacturer conceded, it was outdated and inaccurate, being prone to high readings.[4,5] I am sure that no one involved in the criminal investigation (particularly the Office of the Ontario Chief Coroner) was notified of this very important fact. (If the Office of the Ontario Chief Coroner was notified, then, like other exonerating evidence, the significance was ignored.)

In 1987, in another city, autopsy testing on a blood specimen from a baby who had received only three standard digoxin doses yielded a very high digoxin reading of 70 ngm per mL, confirmed by four different RIA tests.[6] This reading was higher than most of the digoxin readings dealt with in the Grange Inquiry, yet no one suggested digoxin poisoning, particularly murder by intentional digoxin overdosing. Again seriously questioning the validity of RIA test results, the researchers, the Seccombe group, who attributed this very high digoxin reading as being caused by substances read as digoxin by the RIA test method, commented in the *Journal of Forensic Sciences*: "Further studies are required to identify the factors and conditions leading to elevations of DLIS (digoxin-like immunoreactive substances)."[7]

Dr. Seccombe had been one of the expert witnesses in the Grange Inquiry, and he raised the issue of digoxin-like substances interfering with RIA digoxin tests as a source of high RIA digoxin readings. At the time of the Grange Inquiry, Seccombe could show only relatively small elevations in digoxin readings attributable to DLIS, not the 70 ngm per mL mentioned in this 1987 *Journal of Forensic Sciences* article. Since the expected blood level after three standard "loading doses" of digoxin should have been about 1 ngm per mL, this means that in this autopsy blood sample, 69 ngm per mL were not digoxin, but represented a digoxin-imitating substance (a digoxin-like immunoreactive substance, or DLIS).

Unlike what happened when similarly high autopsy digoxin readings were found at the HSC, no one even hinted at murder by digoxin poisoning. The multiple murder theory, which arose from the HSC autopsy findings, seemingly dominated the minds of the Commissioner, the pathologists, the HSC doctors, the Office of the Ontario Chief Coroner and, finally (and understandably) the police. They all seemed blind to any exonerating evidence. Even Dr. Ross Bennett, the Ontario Chief Coroner at the time, remained unconvinced of the poisoning-by-digoxin murder theory until the digoxin reading on the very last baby death (Justin Cook) was revealed.

Although, apparently, Dr. Ross Bennett was not involved, I still suspected that someone else behind the scenes was acting in a role as an advocate for the prosecution, someone who may have been trying to make the Crown's case look good for mass murder of babies by intentional digoxin overdosing.

Another extremely important source of high digoxin measurements is related to the normal storage of digoxin in the heart cells of patients treated with it.

Since my days as an internal medicine resident, I had been aware that the therapeutic blood level of digoxin should be 0.5 to 1.5 ngm per mL, a level that was documented in the GIR on several occasions. The pathologists, pediatricians, cardiac surgeons, and biochemists were alerted to this. It was because of this knowledge that, when my eyes first fell on the 975 ngms per mL as a level that can be normal for the interior of heart muscle cells, it virtually blazed out of the pages, jolting me like a lightning bolt.

Just as all those studying for the medical Fellowship examinations, I had learned that the thin membrane making up the walls of all body cells acts as a living pump that transfers substances in the blood into the cell interior. Heart cells have a particular ability to pump digoxin from the blood into the heart cells' interiors, where it becomes concentrated to levels up to 1,000 times higher within the heart cells' interiors than in the circulating blood. To achieve and maintain such a high concentration of digoxin, these specialized microscopically striated muscle heart cells must be healthy and alive.

I knew that blood samples taken by the pathologists during autopsies for post mortem forensic analysis were usually taken from the heart chambers, or from the great vessels (the aorta or from the body's largest veins, the venae cavae, close to the heart). The heart cells are severely damaged and die within minutes after death. After death, cell membranes of damaged or dead heart cells lose the ability pump digoxin into heart cells and to maintain high intracellular digoxin concentrations. The cell membranes become microscopically porous, allowing the intracellular digoxin to diffuse freely into the blood in the heart and into the adjacent aorta and venae cavae, the sources from which blood for post mortem digoxin testing is extracted.

The high digoxin measurements taken by the pathologists under the direction of the Office of the Ontario Chief Coroner, and recorded in the GIR, were mostly from such sources, being taken up to 15 hours after death. Any pathologist who had recently passed the Fellowship examinations, particularly those with an interest in attending the HSC Mortality Review Committee meetings, should have been aware of the pathophysiological mechanisms that were active in this set of circumstances. University hospitals attract their teaching staff, medical doctors, surgeons, pediatricians, and pathologists based on this depth of knowledge of disease processes.

The digoxin in heart cells before and hours after death would be similar to a sugar cube wrapped in polyethylene, as opposed to being wrapped in tissue paper, and placed in a cup of hot coffee — the polyethylene would prevent the sugar from entering the hot coffee, just as the living heart cell membranes would prevent the digoxin from seeping out into the surrounding blood, while the tissue paper would allow the sugar to diffuse freely into the coffee. Post mortem cell death would convert the heart cell membranes into the equivalent of tissue paper, as far as the stored digoxin is concerned, allowing digoxin at 1,000 times blood levels to diffuse into the blood in the heart and great vessels, the areas from which pathologists take the blood samples for post mortem analysis.

Therefore, compared to the circulating blood digoxin levels in life, even very high digoxin levels were not only possible, but should have been expected, naturally, in blood specimens taken by pathologists in the autopsy rooms hours after death. The pediatricians, cardiologists, and cardiac surgeons and the pathologists, particularly those with very recent training for the Canadian Fellowship examinations, should have been particularly aware of this sequence of events. It was very obvious to me, a diagnostic radiologist, exactly because of such training.

All the digoxin readings interpreted as representing intentional digoxin poisoning were taken by a pathologist in the autopsy room hours after death. One case that is especially noteworthy, J.E., had the blood sample taken over 15 hours after death.[8,9] In J.E.'s particular case, in these long-delayed autopsy samples for digoxin assay, "one pathologist drew blood from a leg artery while his colleague squeezed the leg muscles, drawing out the blood in a milking-like fashion."[10] It must be emphasized that this sample would not represent the blood chemistry prevailing in life because:

1. The capillary blood was left standing for 15 hours in dead leg muscles (made up of striated muscle cells that are similar to heart cells, both in microscopic appearance, and in their ability to store digoxin) and was being

"milked" out of the muscles' capillaries, into the vessel from which blood was taken (almost wrung out).

2. The sample was not from circulating venous blood of a living patient (the sources from which known standards have been calculated).

Dr. Peter Macklem, an inquiry expert witness, repeatedly, forcefully, and correctly denounced drawing any conclusions about autopsy blood levels, because the normal values were absolutely unknown.

Gross inaccuracies attributable to the RIA test have been documented. Grange should have given more credence to the original opinions of the panel of attending physicians that the deaths were from natural causes, opinions that became swayed by the interpretation of specimens taken by a pathologist in an autopsy room of the hospital. Despite my apprehension that someone behind the scenes was stridently promoting the murder-by-digoxin-poisoning theory, Grange, as a judge, should have recognized the grossness of the disparities in the RIA digoxin readings on the same autopsy blood sample of K.P. in three different laboratories, the HSC, the Centre of Forensic Sciences, and Mount Sinai Hospital (26 ngm, 26 ngm, and 112 ngm, respectively).

As well as the erratic, high-reading RIA tests, there was the HPLC (high performance liquid chromatography) digoxin test method to consider. It was introduced because of the high degree of accuracy anticipated by Dr. Cimbura of the Centre of Forensic Sciences. MBT, which could be found in the pharmaceutical rubber in disposable syringes, IV apparatus, and even in the rubber stoppers of the test tubes used to transfer the blood samples to the laboratory, could cause falsely high digoxin readings by the HPLC test method,[11] which became the major test method used by the CFS laboratory to obtain digoxin "readings." This issue will be discussed in Chapter Twenty.

Nineteen

A Contaminant Can Be Measured As Digoxin

In the quest for answers in what was erroneously called intentional digoxin poisoning, a surreal twist of statistical improbability descended on the scene surrounding the digoxin poisoning drama.

In the middle of the HSC baby death period, a feeling of foreboding hung around the cardiac wards of the HSC. At the same time, a perplexing problem had surfaced in the laboratory of the FDA's National Center for Drug Analysis in St. Louis, Missouri. Enigmatically, as Yvonne Juhl was performing routine random testing of drug samples in unit dose form, to make sure the dose measuring had been accurate, excessively high dioxin readings were found in the unit dose delivery systems for the heart drug digoxin. These were random samples of precisely measured doses of digoxin in syringe/needle prepackaged sterile form. The whole purpose of this dose delivery system was to guarantee not only sterility, but to ensure that correct doses of digoxin would be delivered to patients. The test method being used for digoxin assays was the HPLC (high performance liquid chromatography) method. The FDA laboratories believed that the HPLC test was far more accurate than the RIA (radio-immunoassay) test that was most commonly used.

She was greatly disturbed at the digoxin content, which was much higher than indicated on the packages.

The first variable she examined was the preloading of the unit dose digoxin at the factory. She examined the factory loading apparatus, finding it was performing perfectly.

She then focused her attention on the HPLC test method. To her surprise, it was the highly respected HPLC test method that was at fault. Further research proved that an unsuspected contaminant, MBT, from the natural rubber plunger tip of the unit dose syringe had leached into the digoxin solution. Astonishingly, MBT was being read as digoxin by this highly touted HPLC test.[1,2]

The contaminant, MBT, was a catalyst used in the vulcanization process to convert latex into natural rubber. Her research showed that it was known both as an allergen and as a toxin.

This discovery was in the same time frame as the Australian finding that toxic MBT, leaching from syringe rubber, was the cause of human cell deaths in laboratory cultures worldwide.

MBT is a two-headed dragon. The one head can kill by being a cumulative toxin — the more often MBT contaminated injections are administered, the higher the blood levels of MBT — and the greater the toxic effects. This was during the HSC baby death period, and MBT entering the blood of the HSC babies would be measured as digoxin by the HPLC test method (introduced by the Centre for Forensic Sciences because of its great accuracy).

The other head can kill rapidly by anaphylaxis. Juhl's discovery was at the same time as the cluster of allergic reactions with anaphylaxis from MBT contamination occurred in my office practice.

It was coincident also with the startling finding of MBT compounds at "potentially toxic" levels in 91 neonatal babies in London, England.[3] The uncommon term, benzothiazolethiolate (BTT) was used, effectively disguising that the source of the poisoning was MBT, mercaptobenzothiazole. "Thio-" and "mercapto-" can be used interchangeably, but MBT remains by far the term in most common usage.

The dramatic discovery of an allergenic poison contaminating the contents of 50 percent of syringes did not result in warnings to the medical profession. It resulted in no recalls of unit-dose syringes (or other syringes which were equally affected worldwide). This significant medical hazard discovered by Health and Human Services' national drug testing laboratory wasn't published in the *Journal of the American Medical Association*, or in the *New England Journal*. It was sidelined into a pharmacology journal, seldom read — or even cited — by physicians. It did not get the national and international news headlines it deserved.

The information was thus effectively suppressed — almost as if it had been censored. Current supplies of contaminated drugs in unit dose form were used up on patients (medical patients, and dental patients through unit dose dental local anesthetic). Anaphylactic reactions and deaths were invariably assigned to the injected pharmaceutical because the presence of an allergenic contaminant, MBT, was absolutely unsuspected.

Similarly, the cumulative toxic effects associated with repeated injections were assigned to other causes (such as to digoxin toxicity at the HSC) or were classified as of unknown etiology (as the liver damage occurring in premature infants on continuous intravenous feeding, using syringe pumps with large calibre syringes that are larger than the infants' thighs). Cumulative MBT toxicity is a known cause of liver damage.[4]

Further analyses revealed that similar MBT leaching occurred from the pharmaceutical natural rubber components of 50 percent of the disposable syringes in unit dose form. Because similar natural rubber was in disposable plastic syringes around the world, the problem was global. Furthermore, Juhl's discovery indicated that any digoxin blood samples taken in 1981, using disposable syringes with natural rubber plunger parts, would have had a 50 percent chance of being contaminated with significant amounts of MBT, which would be measured as digoxin by the HPLC test.

Dr. Cimbura of the Centre of Forensic Sciences started using the HPLC test method for digoxin testing of HSC autopsy blood samples in 1981. Its introduction was expected to usher in a new level of confidence in the accuracy of the digoxin testing, overcoming the high reading inaccuracy inherent in the RIA test. The HSC's notoriously inaccurate Beckman RIA test had been relied upon to get readings of the digoxin levels in post mortem specimens!

If, at the time of the HSC baby death epidemic, appropriate public health attention had been directed at the pervasive presence of, and the major medical significance of MBT contamination of injections as health protection agency warnings in world medical journals, in international newspapers, and in radio and television newscasts, someone might have linked two separate yet intimately interconnected baby poisoning epidemics on two continents. These were the baby poisoning epidemic in London, England at the Hammersmith Hospital from 1981 to 1982 by MBT compounds, and the Toronto HSC baby poisoning epidemic. They were taking place at exactly the same time. I believe Dr. Napke might have made the MBT connection in 1982, instead of 1987. The Grange Inquiry might not have come into existence, at least as part of a mass murder investigation, because no one, no matter how persistent or persuasive, could have convinced others that there were murders at the HSC.

There was indeed an epidemic of poisoning at the Toronto Hospital for Sick Children in 1980 and 1981. However, that poisoning was not from digoxin and certainly not from intentional digoxin over-dosage by the nursing staff. The poisoning was not by murderous intent, but from contamination of injections by MBT leaching from natural rubber contact — insidious, unsuspected, and unintentional.

Unfortunately, it was not until 1993 that the connections between MBT's unsuspected presence — as a rubber contaminant of injections, as a source of widespread toxicity, and as a cause of falsely high digoxin readings — was brought out in the open. An article, featured on the cover of the *Canadian Nurse Journal*, made the front pages of newspapers across Canada as it came off the presses and was a dominant component of television newscasts nationally.[5]

Because MBT leached out of syringe rubber parts of 50 percent of the syringes tested by the FDA at this time, MBT would have been a common contaminant of autopsy blood samples taken by the Centre of Forensic Sciences (CFS), leading to false elevations in digoxin readings by HPLC, one of the two digoxin testing methods used by the CFS — and MBT could leach into the contents of the CFS test tubes from their natural rubber stoppers. MBT could be added to the test material when a disposable syringe was used again to transfer the test tube contents to the HPLC test apparatus.

Twenty

A Worldwide Epidemic of Poisoning

Natural rubber is a remarkable substance from which one can create bouncing balls or blimps, elastic bands or electric wire insulators, automobile tires, or seals of pharmaceutical ampoules and intravenous and blood transfusion bottles.

Charles Goodyear invented the modern process of creating natural rubber from latex (vulcanization) in 1839. He discovered that raw latex, which could be stretched like bread dough, could be converted into a remarkably tough and durable form that could be stretched in any direction without breaking, or compressed in any direction without losing its original shape when the compression was removed. The manufacturing process of vulcanization required a catalyst (an accelerator) to generate cross-linkages between all the adjacent, very long, spring-like latex molecules, creating a strong spring-like action in every direction, in all planes, thus creating the natural rubber with which we are all familiar.

Tough, durable, elastic, natural rubber, which required 2-mercaptobenzothiazole (MBT) as a catalyst (accelerator), was in common use for medical rubber applications in the 1960s and in almost universal use in the 1970s and 1980s and — in some notable instances — into the 21st century.[1] This natural rubber was in contact with injected pharmaceuticals and injected fluids because its rubber properties were useful in the compliant tips of the plungers of disposable plastic syringes, as the seals for drug ampoules, as the stoppers in the inverted glass bottles for intravenous fluid administration and blood transfusion sets, and in other components of intravenous administration sets. Commonly, in the same patient, all of these factors were operating simultaneously during one single intravenous administration process (e.g. injecting a drug using a disposable syringe with a natural rubber plunger part, from a natural rubber sealed ampoule, into a rubberized sideline of an intravenous fluid or blood transfusion administration set, running from an inverted natural rubber stoppered bottle).

As early as 1969, because MBT was being used in the manufacture of pharmaceutical rubber in disposable syringes, ampoule seals, and parts of intravenous apparatus, Guess and O'Leary examined it in the laboratory, showing its toxicity and its damaging effects on embryos. They warned that both H-MBT and MBT were "highly toxic in mice,"[2] particularly in causing acute liver damage (toxic hepatitis), and that the MBT was even more dangerous because it became more toxic as it accumulated in the body when repeated injections were required. One should pay particular attention to these two features concerning the HSC baby poisoning deaths, not as it applies to poisoning by digoxin, but about the possibility of cumulative poisoning by MBT compounds.

Because this type of pharmaceutical natural rubber was in widespread use, its tendency to cause liver damage was probably an unsuspected major factor in the liver damage known to develop in premature infants on continuous intravenous feeding. Infusion pumps used 20 or 50 mL syringes containing rubber plunger parts that were large compared to the size of the babies.[3,4] Just as Lasser's group showed a marked drop in the incidence of reactions to X-ray dyes after 1990,[5] when MBT rubber was no longer being used in syringes and in ampoule seals, a similar study of the incidence of liver damage in neonates on total parenteral intravenous nutrition after 1990 will show a similar significant drop if it is related to MBT toxicity.

The Guess and O'Leary study, although arising from within a laboratory, rather than a clinical setting, noted that pediatric digoxin, unlike most pharmaceuticals, used alcohol as a solvent. Since MBT, as well as digoxin, is far more soluble in alcohol than in the water that is used to dissolve most pharmaceuticals, Guess and O'Leary made the prophetic observation (regarding infant cardiac patients), that this "may have one of its most serious implications in infant therapy."[6] This conclusion was drawn because they realized that syringes of the same size were used for small babies and for adults. MBT was particularly toxic to the liver, causing chemical hepatitis, a cause of nausea and vomiting. Thus, in 1969, they concluded that any MBT contamination of injections from pharmaceutical rubber would have been delivering relatively much larger doses of toxic MBT compounds into the bodies of babies who were already quite ill from the diseases being treated.

Although, in 1985, Meek and Pettit were discussing H-MBT in the following statement, it applies equally to MBT, as shown in the Guess and O'Leary mice studies in 1969: H-MBT "may accumulate in patients who receive several injections while in hospital or in patients who are on constant parenteral (intravenous) medication."[7] Just imagine how this would apply to seriously ill hospital patients who would receive many injections of pharmaceuticals.

This aspect of MBT compound toxicity is demonstrated best in a direct quote from their article (which echoed the 1969 similar sentiments of Guess and O'Leary): "The inadvertent administration of H-MBT may be of particular importance in hospitalized infants, especially premature infants, children and patients with impaired elimination."

This statement would apply to the HSC babies, particularly those on Ward 4B, who were more seriously ill. As well as the syringes and ampoule natural rubber seals, intravenous therapy would be administering leached MBT from three different sites — the large rubber stopper in the inverted glass bottle containing the IV fluid, the rubber float valve, and the rubber side line into which a nurse can inject intravenous medications.

In 1981, during the HSC baby death epidemic, but on the other side of the world, Petersen et al[8] published a Brief Communication in the *Australia and New Zealand Journal of Medicine*, followed later by a much more comprehensive article, warning of the contamination of injectable drugs in disposable syringes by H-MBT (hydroxyethyl-mercapto-benzothiazole) leaching from the rubber tips of syringe plungers.[9] They showed that the toxicity of MBT compounds was responsible for the death of human embryo cells in cultures occurring in laboratories around the world during the time when disposable plastic syringes were being used. Unfortunately, this detailed article was published in the *Journal of Pharmaceutical Sciences*, which is not often read or referred to by practicing physicians.

They showed that when the rubber plunger parts in these syringes containing MBT were sterilized using ethylene oxide gas (the commonest method of syringe sterilization), H-MBT was formed. This H-MBT was found to interfere with the measurement of the blood level of hydrocortisone, leading to falsely high measurements of hydrocortisone in patients being monitored for the therapeutic level of this drug.

They reported that some of the MBT remained unchanged by the sterilization and also leached from rubber parts of the syringe plungers, contaminating the syringe's fluid contents.

The cumulative toxicity of MBT compounds is very pertinent in the examination of the cause of the increased HSC baby deaths. There was a higher death rate on Ward 4B, where the babies were generally much sicker and therefore would require significantly more injections of drugs and IV fluids. Thus, there would be much more exposure to the cumulative toxin, MBT. Compounding this is the obvious observation that a very ill baby would be more apt to die when poisoned, and that baby would be much harder to resuscitate when a cardiac arrest occurred — particularly if the cardiac arrest was due to poisoning by MBT compounds.

Even small 2 mL syringes leached significant amounts of MBT compounds, 2 micrograms of H-MBT in five minutes. The amount of H-MBT leached was not related much to the amount of fluid in the syringe, but increased directly in proportion to the surface area of the syringe plungers. One must realize therefore that a syringe that is two times the diameter of another will leach four times as much MBT. Also, with blood digoxin analysis, which is measured in nanograms (0.5 to 1.5 nanograms per mL is the therapeutic blood level), the 2 micrograms of the leached MBT compound will be 2,000 nanograms. (Normal blood digoxin levels should be no more than 1.5 nanograms per cc of blood.)

Petersen's group issued an almost omniscient warning, that this finding of MBT compounds "has implications extending from possible interference with analyses required for pathological tests or therapeutic monitoring, to the possibility of acute and/ or chronic toxicity." This certainly has strong implications in the Toronto baby poisoning deaths in both ways, interference with analytical tests and the poisoning of babies, which resulted in an increased death rate.

Another Epidemic of Baby Poisoning

Of undeniably great significance to the understanding of the probable cause of the HSC baby poisoning deaths was a discovery an ocean away at the time of the HSC baby-poisoning epidemic

Hammersmith Hospital, in London, England, is a major teaching hospital, associated with the Imperial College Medical Faculty. On a neonatal ward of this hospital, Meek and Pettit were studying the therapeutic blood concentration of the drug, theophylline. An unexpected concentration spike of an unknown chemical was detected in electrophoresis graphs of the analysis of the blood chemistry of babies.[10] Further analysis showed this compound was C-MBT, or carboxyethyl-MBT (Meek and Pettit called it CMB), a compound that had originated as MBT from natural rubber parts of syringes, drug ampoules, and IV apparatus.

In all, they found 91 babies with "potentially toxic levels of this MBT compound."

Pumps, using relatively very large syringes (50 mL) were in frequent use for total parenteral nutrition for premature babies.

The Meek and Pettit study involved only babies monitored for theophylline, but any other babies in any London hospital wards who were getting multiple injections would have similarly "potentially toxic" C-MBT levels. So also would any babies on any children's hospital ward anywhere in the world, Paris, New York, Montreal — and Toronto (at the Hospital for Sick Children), during this period of study in the early 1980s.

This was at the same time that Yvonne Juhl, at the U.S. National Center for Drug Analysis, had found, incidentally, contamination of digoxin by MBT in unit dose syringes, through contamination by pharmaceutical rubber.

The Hammersmith Hospital H-MBT was proven to have originated as MBT, which they termed BTT, or benzothiazolethiolate, a catalyst required in the manufacture of the natural rubber components of syringes, rubber sealing caps

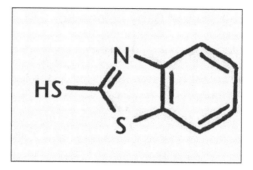

Figure 6

on drug ampoules, and rubber components of intravenous and blood transfusion apparatus. This MBT had been converted to H-MBT during the sterilization process, using ethylene oxide gas. In the babies' bodies, the H-MBT had been converted to C-MBT.

The Hammersmith investigators used "CMB," instead of C-MBT and "benzothiazolethiolate," instead of mercaptobenzothiazole. This substitution of "thio" for "mercapto" disguised the MBT nature of the "CMB" contamination from the prying eyes of MBT researchers, like me, before computer searches of the literature were possible, causing this extremely important and very pertinent article to remain inaccessible. It was discovered fortuitously in 1992. The differing (and relatively unusual) but chemically correct terminology can be seen in the following diagram of the chemical structure of these MBT compounds (see Figure 6). Figure 7 is the chemical structure diagram as shown in textbooks.

This is MBT, where X = H. It is a mirror image of the diagram above, when one replaces the H with an X. There is a C at each corner of the hexagon (which is a benzene ring). There is another C at the trifurcation point in the centre of the N, the S, and the SH.

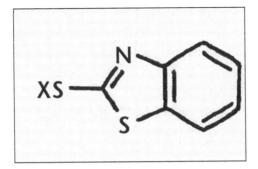

Figure 7

MBT (BTT, Meek and Pettit): X = H
H-MBT (HEB, Meek and Pettit): X = CH2-CH2-COOH
C-MBT (CMB, Meek and Pettit): X = CH2-COOH

MBT = Mercapto-benzo-thiazole
= 2-Benzo-thiazole-thiolate
= BTT (Meek and Pettit)

H-MBT = 2-2(Hydroxyethyl)-mercapto-benzo-thiazole
= 2,2(Hydroxy-ethylthio)-benzothiazole
= HEB (Meek and Pettit)

C-MBT = 2-(carboxymethyl)-mercapto-benzo-thiazole
= (Carboxy-methylthio)-benzothiazole
= CMB (Meek and Pettit)
Hyphens have been used to clarify the origins of the terms.

It must be emphasized that Meek and Pettit were studying only babies taking one drug, theophylline. Because the MBT originated in the pharmaceutical rubber of syringes, ampoule seals, and IV apparatus, similar MBT levels would be found in any babies receiving multiple injections of any drugs, or intravenous fluids, or blood — anywhere in the industrialized world.

Thus, the extremely important Hammersmith baby-poisoning epidemic caused by MBT compounds was masked by the choice of terminology, CMB.

Meek and Pettit reported their findings of MBT compound contamination in the *Lancet*.[11] They described how H-MBT ("HEB") was a cumulative toxin (the blood concentration gradually built up with repeated exposure) and that the H-MBT was changed into C-MBT ("CMB") in the babies' bodies. The repeated intravenous administration of this pharmaceutical rubber resulted in "potentially toxic" levels of MBT compounds in 91 babies.

The use of the much less common term BTT for MBT would keep this MBT poisoning article under the radar of researchers — almost like a kind of low-tech stealth technology — which allowed this vitally important discovery to escape the pages of newspapers and the notice of practicing physicians worldwide.

Thus, an epidemic of MBT compound poisoning was occurring at the exactly the same time as Toronto HSC babies were apparently dying from what was also termed by Grange as a poisoning epidemic. The same toxic pharmaceutical rubber contaminants must have been injected, in at least the same amounts, into the sickest cardiac patients at the HSC — the patients located on ward 4B, because the sickest babies would require more injections of drugs, IV fluids, and blood.

If the same electrophoresis biochemistry graphs had been made of the blood chemistry of wards of sick patients (adults and children) across the industrialized world at this time, the same spike of a mysterious poison, an MBT compound, would have been found. The conditions that Meek and Pettit describe that resulted in these "potentially toxic" levels of H-MBT in the Hammersmith neonatal babies, were present in every children's hospital ward in every country in the world — in London,

Paris, Boston, Montreal, Toronto — the same medical rubber and the same sterilization method were in almost universal use — a pandemic (worldwide epidemic) of poisoning that was insidious, unsuspected, undiagnosed, and untreated.

Yes, the sickest HSC babies (those on Ward 4B) were being poisoned, but not by digoxin, but by MBT compounds, just as the Hammersmith babies were being poisoned at exactly the same time. The poisoning and deaths of babies on the cardiac wards at the HSC by cumulative MBT poisoning were being erroneously and invariably attributed to poisoning by digoxin. In much the same way, the worldwide allergic reactions to MBT in injections were invariably attributed to allergy to the injected pharmaceutical (the dentist's local anesthetic, the influenza immunization vaccine, the insulin, the radio-opaque X-ray dyes).

As early as 1969, Guess and O'Leary,[12] aware of MBT's widespread use in the manufacture of natural rubber used in syringes and in pharmaceutical vial seals, studied its toxicity in laboratory animals. The cumulative toxic effect of MBT compounds showed particular toxicity to the liver, inducing a chemical hepatitis. A significant clinical finding in chemical hepatitis would be, just as with viral hepatitis A, nausea and vomiting. Babies would be much more vulnerable than adults to leached MBT effects because the same IV sets, syringes, and ampoule seals were being used — and babies would be getting a far larger relative dose because of their small size. The Grange Inquiry Report repeatedly mentioned nausea and vomiting as a characteristic feature of digoxin poisoning.

The MBT-induced liver toxicity would make the HSC babies sicker, and they would require more IV fluids and medication, thus allowing even more MBT exposure, and they would become even sicker still. A poisoned very sick baby would be more likely to die than a baby who had not been so ill, and a baby poisoned in this way would be far harder, if not impossible, to resuscitate than if only cardiac complications were involved.

The National Center for Drug Analysis showed its results that 50 percent of pharmaceutical rubber used in syringes, IV apparatus, pharmaceutical ampoule rubber, leached significant amounts of MBT, again at the exact time of the HSC baby poisoning deaths. Digoxin, dissolved in alcohol in which MBT is particularly soluble,[13] must have been involved in any MBT cumulative toxicity in the HSC baby cardiac patients, when digoxin was being administered by injection. One can hear the prophetic words of Guess and O'Leary resonating in the background that MBT, dissolved with the injected fluids or drugs, "may have one of its most serious implications in infant therapy."[14]

During an exchange of letters with me, Professor Charles B. Airaudo, of Marseilles, France, a pharmacologist and the world authority on MBT compounds contaminating pharmaceuticals, explained that C-MBT is a metabolite (changed by the body after entering the circulation) of H-MBT, and that H-MBT is formed when pharmaceutical rubber, manufactured with MBT as an accelerator, is sterilized by ethylene oxide gas, as is usually done.[15]

Meek and Pettit commented correctly that babies were especially vulnerable to the leaching of toxic MBT because of their small size and because the same size syringes and rubber-containing IV apparatus were used as for adults. A geometric factor, the surface area of rubber contact, came into play in this contamination, especially when large 50 mL syringes were used in infusion pumps for infant intravenous nutrition. Some of the HSC babies had received such intravenous feeding and medication by the syringe infusion pump route.

Thus, what has been discussed is the leaching of MBT from the MBT-rubber components of various medical devices into injected fluids. MBT is moderately water-soluble, but it is very soluble in alcohol. Consider these facts:

1. Injectable digoxin uses alcohol as a solvent.
2. MBT would contaminate injected digoxin from ampoule seals.
3. MBT would contaminate digoxin from rubber seals of syringes used to inject.
4. MBT would enter the babies' blood with digoxin.
5. MBT is a cumulative toxin — each exposure adds to the previous — increasing its concentration in the blood (Guess and O'Leary, 1969, in mice; Meek and Pettit, 1980–1983 in Hammersmith Hospital babies).

If the Hammersmith poisoning had been from arsenic in pharmaceutical rubber and arsenic had been found in 50 percent of pharmaceutical rubber samples, as MBT was,[16] this revelation would have made headlines, worldwide, not just for a day or two, but for weeks on end, until the media were assured that arsenic had been eradicated from the rubber manufacturing process.

However, this poison was not arsenic though, like arsenic, MBT exerted a cumulative poisoning effect. MBT's breakdown products in the body (such as C-MBT) built up in the blood with repeated exposure, as in the Hammersmith babies. This allergenic poison was prevalent around the world, in disposable plastic syringes, in unit dose syringes in which a measured dose of a drug is in contact with MBT rubber for up to three years, in the rubber seals on ampoules of pharmaceuticals, in the stoppers in intravenous bottles, and in blood transfusion sets.

It seems that when hospital laboratories and the laboratories of health protection agencies encountered and recognized MBT contaminants, they were somehow encouraged to soft pedal it — even, perhaps, disguise its nature (e.g. my experience with "a phenolic compound"), so that MBT was allowed to remain, like an invisible spectre that sometimes is depicted carrying a scythe (the "Grim Reaper"), in the background of pertinent medical knowledge. As a result, these injection-related, natural-rubber-containing medical products were not removed from the marketplace. Instead, despite knowledge of their danger, they were permitted to be used up on patients, worldwide, while more were being manufactured.Except for the 91 Hammersmith babies in London, England, almost all the poisonings worldwide were attributed to the disease processes being treated or, in the case of the HSC baby deaths, incorrectly attributed to digoxin over-dosage. In a similar way, except for two isolated instances in my office, the severe allergic reactions and deaths from MBT contaminants invariably were attributed to allergy to the pharmaceutical being injected, because of the ignorance of MBT's pervasive presence as an allergen in injections.

Twenty-One

Different Death Rates on HSC Cardiac Ward 4A and Ward 4B

Ted Bissland, a dedicated journalist, and a 20-year veteran reporter for the CBC who had become a specialist on legal affairs, religiously attended the hearings and the Grange Inquiry sessions, making voluminous notes that ended up compressed into a chronicle of the testimony that Grange heard, and it has become a permanent record of some of Grange's comments, in his book: *Death Shift: The Digoxin Murders at Sick Kids.*[1]

Bissland's research revealed that, in the spring of 1980, the HSC cardiac patients were all moved to two adjacent wards, 4A and 4B, each with its own supervising nursing teams. It was 4B on which the high death rate was occurring.

He described that the post-cardiac-surgery patients (with a naturally expected higher than normal death rate) were on Ward 4B. Also, 4B held "those whom the hospital was trying to stabilize prior to surgery; in some of these cases it would be classified as heroic surgery," in which chances of survival were quite low, with or without surgery. Nevertheless, if these infants survived the surgery, their health and lives would be improved vastly, making the risk of surgery worthwhile.

Thus, under normal circumstances, many of these 4B patients would be critically ill, with a significantly higher probability of dying than the average cardiac patient, such as those on ward 4A, and would be far more difficult to resuscitate when they developed a cardiac arrest. In addition, such seriously ill patients, when poisoned by MBT leached from medical rubber, would be more apt to die than the less frail patients on ward 4A.

Because they were more critically ill, the 4B babies would require more injections, more intravenous fluids, and more transfusions. Thus, probably they would be getting at least as much exposure to toxic MBT compounds as the Hammersmith babies, in whom MBT compounds had reached "potentially toxic" levels, in exactly this period. For these reasons, the death rate on 4B, the ward to which Susan Nelles just happened to be assigned, should have been expected to be significantly higher than on 4A.

Thus, we have learned that MBT leaching into injections is indeed a two-headed dragon. One head causes severe allergic reactions, anaphylaxis, and deaths, as described in Part I of this book, and the other head causes disease and can kill as a cumulative toxin.

1) It was two series of clustered reactions with life-threatening anaphylaxis, in 1983 and in 1986, which were related to contamination of X-ray radiopaque dyes by MBT. Similar syringes and similar anaphylaxis and deaths were occurring all over the world — from injecting any drug — any systemic administration of dental local anesthetics, insulin, immunization vaccines, etc. It was only because of these severe allergic reactions in London, Ontario, that MBT contaminations of injections came to light in a clinical setting — the only two reports of allergic reactions to unsuspected leached MBT in injections

resulting in anaphylaxis in the world medical literature. From 1980 to 1983, 50 percent of syringe rubber leached significant MBT into the drug being injected.[2]

2) MBT can kill as a cumulative poison. Coincident with the FDA's 50-percent finding, 91 babies who were being monitored for just one drug, theophylline, demonstrated an unexpected peak in the electrophoresis pattern of the their blood chemistry. The chemical was an MBT compound (they called the contaminant BTT (benzothiazolethiolate), an uncommonly used chemical name for MBT (mercaptobenzothiazole). This MBT compound increased in concentration with repeated exposures (repeated injections). MBT was particularly damaging to the liver, because it was entering the circulation faster than it was excreted. Although Meek and Pettit noted that the MBT compound had reached "potentially toxic levels," they failed to emphasize that similar poisoning must have been occurring in every pediatric hospital ward in every city, in every country in the developed world — wherever and whenever babies were subjected to frequent injections of medications, IV fluids, or blood, with repeated exposure to MBT leaching into injections.

Again, at this same time (1980–1981), an epidemic of "baby poisoning" (the exact wording used by Grange in his Inquiry Report) was occurring on the cardiac wards 4A and 4B of the Toronto Hospital for Sick Children, resulting in an increased death rate. The babies on nurse Susan Nelles's ward, 4B, were sicker, and therefore received many more injections.

Twenty-Two

An Epidemic of Infant Cardiac Deaths across Canada

Acting on a suspicion that some unknown but widespread factor was responsible for the increased cardiac ward baby deaths at the HSC, Dr. Albert Burton, Professor of Biochemistry at UBC, studied Statistics Canada data to compare baby cardiac deaths nationally at the time of the HSC baby death epidemic. This was a stroke of genius in its utter simplicity. Burton proved that a similar infant cardiac death pattern was occurring in most provinces across Canada during this time. Investigative journalists Kinsella and MacLeod of the *Ottawa Citizen* quoted Professor Burton, who subjected the digoxin poisoning theory to serious scrutiny, even to ridicule, by stating, "Clearly, one has to stretch the mysterious poisoner theory to the limits of absurdity, or concede that what happened at the HSC was happening nationwide."[1] Like almost everyone at the time, Professor Burton was unaware of MBT.

The global scope of baby cardiac deaths at this time was not examined by Burton, or he might have said that what was happening at the HSC was happening worldwide, an epidemic of poisoning, but not from digoxin. Although the same conditions prevailed around the world, poisoning by MBT was recognized only on one ward, a neonatal ward, in one hospital, Hammersmith Hospital in England. Professor Burton used the kind of approach to statistical analysis that should have been expected from the staff of the Atlanta Centers for Disease Control, who were the experts on epidemiology, but they were misled, reaching the incorrect conclusions that became a part of the Grange Inquiry Report.

With a good measure of confidence, one can suggest now that Burton's "mysterious poisoner" wasn't a person at all, but an unsuspected "mysterious toxin," the Hammersmith toxin, the insidious contaminant, MBT, or an MBT derivative compound. Furthermore, extrapolating Professor Burton's comment to include the whole world, we can explain the true enormity of the poisoning, and that does not even touch on the subject of the many deaths that occurred from anaphylaxis because of allergy to MBT, or to latex.

During the Grange Inquiry, even without access to Professor Burton's statistical analysis and his conclusions, similar sentiments on the digoxin poisoning theory had been expressed in Dr. Peter Macklem's firm condemnation of parts of the murder by digoxin theory: "All reasonable people will reject the conclusions of the Attorney-General's Office that exhumed babies were murdered by digitalis [digoxin] overdose because the evidence upon which this conclusion is based is not valid." (GIR, page 31) Dr. Macklem was a world-recognized medical scientist at McGill.

———

Notwithstanding, an innocent young nurse was accused of murder and had been unjustly imprisoned, before being released on $50,000 bail.

The Terms of Reference for Commissioner Grange dictated that the GIR should have been only a fact-finding exercise. His mandate was not to assign blame, directly or indirectly by inference. In an inquiry, there should have been no place to say, as Grange did: "I may eventually be proven wrong, because the toxicological evidence upon which I in part based my conclusion may be proved wrong or inadequate." As it now appears, Grange exposed himself to justified criticism in both of these categories, something that would have been impossible if he had adhered (as he should have) to the Terms of Reference of the Inquiry.

Twenty-Three

The *Canadian Nurse* Journal Successfully Challenges the Digoxin Poisoning Theory

By 1993, enough convincing evidence had been amassed to show that there were no murders at the HSC, so it was written up as a journal article. I considered what route might be taken to get it published. Because it revealed that pharmaceutical companies had sold, knowingly and worldwide, injectable pharmaceuticals that were in contact with MBT/latex natural rubber, I realized that a physician-based medical journal would be loath to publish it. These journals receive critical revenue from funding by the advertising of drug companies. Twice already, articles requested of me by members of the editorial boards on this subject had not appeared in print.

I thought of the *Canadian Nurse* journal, the journal of the Canadian Nursing Association, feeling that, since this article revolved around an issue central to the nursing profession, they might decide to print it. Initially, the editor, Heather Broughton, felt considerable unease with a story over a decade old — a story told not by a nurse, or a lawyer, or a pediatrician, but by a radiologist from a small private office. However, when some insight was given into the validity of the arguments being presented, the editorial staff of *Canadian Nurse* looked at the written material and the validating references, and put their hearts and souls into cross checking the facts, editing, and refining the article to suit their journal and preparing the layout for publication, feeling justifiably proud of their final result.

All their hard work was rewarded, with the edited article presenting the facts clearly and fairly and with a striking portrayal of the subject matter featured on the cover. The article was accompanied by a thoughtful editorial, "A Theory of Innocence," by Broughton, the editor-in-chief. The media were alerted to the contents just as it was released from the publisher.

On the day of its publication in December 1993, the article, "The Nurses are Innocent,"[1] made the front pages of newspapers across Canada and was featured in the national news of the major television networks, detailing some of the causes for the high digoxin readings and suggesting the real cause of the increased deaths. It explained that the HSC epidemic of poisoning was from the toxic effects of MBT compounds and was similar to the poisonings at Hammersmith Hospital, as described in an article in the *Lancet*.[2]

When the media confronted the Ontario Chief Coroner, Dr. James Young, with the revelations in the *Canadian Nurse* article, he dismissed them offhand by saying, "Hamilton's theory is full of holes." He did not, however, give a single example of a hole, because there was none then, nor is there one now. It was obvious that the Office of the Chief Coroner of Ontario continued to be blind to any evidence that disputed the validity of the deeply entrenched digoxin poisoning theory.

In 1994, with some additional information contained in a personal letter to me from Dr. David Seccombe, Professor of Clinical Chemistry at UBC, a full page article in the *Lawyers*

Weekly[3] (the newspaper of the Canadian legal profession) expanded on some points in the *Canadian Nurse Journal* article, appearing as "It's Time for Justice for the Sick Kids Nurses," under the heading of "Opening Statement." All the lawyers and judges involved in the HSC baby death investigation and in the inquiries would have been exposed to this article, and the heading "Opening Statement" invited challenges from the readers. The editors of the *Lawyers Weekly* received not a single letter of criticism.

My friend, Gordon Killeen, the very learned and highly respected judge in London, Ontario, confided that, in terms of jurisprudence, when an article such as this is exposed to the legal profession in general, and the judiciary in particular, and goes unchallenged, it becomes the final word on the subject. As you will learn in the concluding paragraphs of what you are now reading, the awards committee of Queen's University agreed.

I received a congratulatory call from Professor R.I. Martin of UWO's Law School about the *Lawyers Weekly* article. I remarked that the article was just a very brief summary from my files, some of which might be of interest to the law school. A few minutes after hanging up, I received a call from the Director of the UWO Law Library, asking if the library could have some copies from my records. As a result, I spent a weekend going through my material, selecting pertinent writings to photocopy. There is now a file at the library of the UWO Law School on the Susan Nelles case with carefully selected excerpts from these files — an open source of research material for anyone interested in this case.

Twenty-Four

A Summary of the Case Against the Digoxin Poisoning Theory

A List of Points against Digoxin Poisoning in the HSC Epidemic of Baby Deaths

1. Inaccurate RIA tests: the errors were always on the high side. The HSC's Beckman RIA test was among the worst, being taken off the market just after the GIR, because it was outdated and inaccurate (according to the manufacturer.)

2. The RIA test can read DLIS (digoxin-like-immunoreactive substances) in the blood as digoxin. The 69 ngms per mL of the 70 ngms per mL digoxin reading were DLIS in one 1987 Seccombe case (compared to the normal 0.5 to 1.5 ngm per mL for true digoxin).

3. In one of 14 cases of a control group of autopsies of babies who were taking standard daily doses of digoxin, the CFS found one with a digoxin reading of 169.6 — far higher than any in the HSC baby deaths that were

attributed to digoxin poisoning.

4. MBT can be measured falsely as digoxin on HPLC test, the test used by the CFS to confirm high digoxin readings by the high reading RIA tests. Fifty percent of pharmaceutical rubber in 1981 contaminated the syringe contents and IV fluids with MBT.

5. Digoxin tests were being performed for the very first time on autopsy specimens and on exhumed bodies, with no standards from any source with which to compare them.

6. Heart cells store digoxin at levels up to 1,000 times therapeutic blood levels. These cells die minutes after death, releasing this digoxin into the blood in the heart chambers, the aorta, and the vena cava, sites from which HSC post mortem blood samples for digoxin tests were taken, up to 15 hours after death.

7. At HSC Mortality Conferences, the attending physicians and nurses, in every "digoxin poisoning" death, originally had attributed deaths to natural causes.

8. There was a similar pattern of increased baby cardiac deaths across Canada at the time of the HSC baby deaths.

9. At the time of the epidemic of baby poisoning deaths at the HSC, there was an epidemic of poisoning on a neonatal ward in England — poisonous MBT compounds from rubber parts of syringes, drug ampoule rubber seals, rubber parts of IV apparatus, and blood transfusion sets — a pharmaceutical rubber poisoning scenario that was taking place worldwide, insidiously and completely unsuspected.

10. Someone behind the scenes seemed to be stridently driving the digoxin poisoning theory, discounting exonerating evidence — someone unmentioned — but apparently someone with potent persuasive powers over the office of the Ontario Chief Coroner, over the Crown Prosecutors and, ultimately, over Grange.

A final comment, emphasizing that it wasn't the Chief Coroner, Dr. Ross Bennett, who was promoting the intentional poisoning by digoxin, comes from Ted Bissland's book. He includes a direct quote from Dr. Bennett. After learning of the high digoxin reading on the post mortem specimen of Justin Cook, the last of the baby deaths, Dr. Bennett said: "It's the last straw that broke the camel's back. Up until then I couldn't believe there was murder."[1] This statement proves that Dr. Bennett was not the originator or the vigorous promoter of the murder theory. Someone else in the shadows seemed to be driving the murder theory — a theory that arose out of interpretations of specimens taken within the walls of the autopsy rooms of the Toronto Hospital for Sick Children.

We know who else it wasn't: it wasn't the attending doctors or the nurses. They had come to the conclusion that the deaths were from natural causes. It wasn't the police, who were not asked, but told, that there were murders. Someone not evident in Judge Vanek's preliminary hearing, not evident in the Dubin Report on the HSC, and not evident in the Grange Inquiry Report, attracted the attention of the police. In fact, it appeared to be a person not named at all. To me, the driving force for the malicious digoxin poisoning theory seemed to emanate from within the Office of the Chief Coroner of Ontario. It was based on interpretations from the HSC Department of Pathology autopsy rooms.

Someone seemed to be pulling the puppet strings activating the players in this true tragedy of baby deaths and — almost — enacted an utter tragedy for Susan Nelles. The young nurse fought back ferociously, wrenching herself loose from the strings in which she might have become entangled and which might have bound her in prison.

"Fought" is the absolutely precise terminology, because one momentous battle made history in Canadian jurisprudence. In 1989, Susan Nelles Pine won a precedent-setting lawsuit for malicious prosecution against the Ontario Attorney General and his representative, the Crown Attorney.

It was a carefully crafted murder theory that resulted in her being charged with mass murder of very sick babies, being briefly imprisoned and which threatened to destroy her career. It was a murder theory that forced the creation of Judge Vanek's 41-day preliminary hearing as to whether the charges of murder should be allowed. It was a theory that forced the creation of Dubin Inquiry into the Toronto Hospital for Sick Children. It was a theory that mandated the creation of the 17-month Grange Inquiry. It was a theory that inflicted extreme emotional stress on Susan Nelles and her family, with her father dying as he strove to help clear the name of his beloved daughter. It was a headline-grabbing theory of the murder of babies that wreaked havoc and, potentially, could have resulted in an innocent nurse being wrongfully imprisoned for many years for murder. Does this scenario of the misinterpretation of Ontario autopsy findings, resulting in many natural deaths being falsely attributed to murder, conform to a pattern we have all been reading about in the last few years?

Susan resisted relentlessly. Stoically, she endured.

Twenty-Five

False Diagnoses of Baby Poisoning from Interpretations of Autopsy Specimens

The series of HSC cardiac ward baby deaths became defined as murder by intentional digoxin poisoning from interpretations of specimens taken in the HSC autopsy rooms by members of their Department of Pathology. The natural causes for the findings, and even evidence that surfaced that was obviously exonerating, were dismissed.

Post mortem digoxin tests were being done for the first time, and there were no available standards anywhere in the world for comparison, yet it was apparent that the test methods were inaccurate, always being high on the side of toxicity. The interpretation of these inaccurate RIA tests was that toxicity was induced intentionally.

A panel of HSC attending physicians and nurses had already considered the clinical condition of the patients, coming to the carefully discussed opinion that the deaths were from natural causes. However, a murder theory arose out of the autopsy rooms — a theory soon promoted and defended by the Crown prosecutors and by those operating under the aegis of the Office of the Chief Coroner of Ontario.

Dr. Peter Macklem repeatedly recommended that a controlled series of autopsies be done — by taking post mortem blood samples from babies who died while receiving standard therapeutic doses of digoxin, stimulating Dr. George Cimbura of the Centre of Forensic Sciences to undertake such a series while the Grange Commission was still in progress.

Dr. Cimbura's control series of twenty babies who had been receiving standard therapeutic doses of digoxin turned up one astounding result — blood digoxin level reading that was far higher than any in the Grange Inquiry. This exonerating piece of evidence should have destroyed the poisoning-by-digoxin theory.

However, it was ignored. It is apparent that the murder theory overrode all evidence that indicated death from natural causes.

Early on it seemed that someone was driving the murder-by-digoxin theory, in spite of definite evidence to the contrary. I believed that person was within the Office of the Chief Coroner of Ontario, perhaps even the Chief Coroner, Dr. Ross Bennett.

I had written letters to Dr. Bennett and six letters to the Ontario Attorney General, Marion Boyd. The attorney general failed to respond to any of my letters, which contained much of the exonerating evidence. Selected letters may be accessed through a file at the UWO Law Library, which contains copies of documents from my records on the Susan Nelles case, along with copies of my two published articles[1,2] on the HSC baby deaths.

In recent years, a story centreing on a high-profile pediatric pathologist at the Toronto Hospital for Sick Children has been prominent in the news. In June 2005, because of complaints from defense lawyers and judges, the Chief Coroner of Ontario ordered a review of 44 forensic autopsies carried out by Dr. Charles Smith, a pathologist working in the Department of Pathology at the Toronto Hospital for Sick Children since 1980, while also working as a pediatric forensic pathologist on a fee-for-service basis for the Chief Coroner of Ontario. Thirteen of these cases had resulted in criminal charges and convictions. The report, released in April 2007, indicated that there were substantial problems with nearly half of his interpretations — in 20 of the 44 autopsy reports.

In response to these findings, on April 25, 2007, the Government of Ontario, under the Public Inquiries Act, established an Inquiry into Pediatric Forensic Pathology in Ontario. The Honourable Stephen T. Goudge was appointed as the commissioner, the mandate of which "was to conduct a systemic review and an assessment of the policies, procedures, practices, accountability, and oversight mechanisms, quality control measures, practices and institutional arrangements of pediatric forensic pathology in Ontario from 1981 to 2001 as they relate to its practice and use in investigations and criminal proceedings." He was asked to make recommendations to address systemic failings and restore and enhance public confidence in the system.

Justice Goudge examined the records of those doing pediatric forensic pathology across Canada. Dr. Charles Smith's activities as a pathologist working out of an office at the HSC soon became the focal point of the Goudge Inquiry Report, released October 1, 2008.

Dr. Smith was hired as a resident in pathology at the University of Toronto (which included the Toronto Hospital for Sick Children) from 1978 to 1980. In 1980 — which was at the beginning of what was to become known as the digoxin baby poisoning epidemic period, he was hired by the Hospital for Sick Children as an anatomic pathologist — with an expressed keen interest in performing autopsies on children who had died suddenly.

To the dismay of the Toronto Hospital for Sick Children and the criminal justice system of Canada, Justice Goudge determined conclusively that Dr. Smith's interpretations had incorrectly assigned child autopsy findings to murder as the cause of death in twenty cases from 1981 to 2001.

Although Dr. Smith lacked formal forensic pathology training, he quickly assumed the role of a forensic pediatric pathologist, always working out of the pathology department of the HSC. Although untrained in this area, he eagerly filled in as a forensic pathologist — and the Crown attorneys welcomed him as he played this role. Again and again, he bolstered the case for the prosecution in courts of law, with many convictions based on his testimony.

As Justice Goudge noted, he established an intimate (implying even too intimate) working relationship with the Office of the Chief Coroner of Ontario (OCCO).

"Providing Evidence" is a portion of the "Executive Summary" of the Goudge Report from the Office of the Attorney General. It lists ten serious failings concerning the manner in which Dr. Smith presented his evidence in court.

It noted that Dr. Smith failed to understand that his role as an expert was not to support the Crown, but to provide hard evidence. In the summary, he made a pertinent admission that — when his career began in the 1980s — he believed his role was to act as an advocate for the Crown and "make a case look good." This admission is deemed relevant to the baby deaths that the Crown prosecutors were alleging to be murder by digoxin poisoning.

Justice Goudge noted that, in some cases, he made false statements to the court.

In a written submission by the HSC to the Goudge Inquiry, the HSC made the following statement:

> It is the position of Sick Kids that, while Dr. Smith was engaged as an expert in the justice system, he was operating as an independent fee-for-/contractor for the OCCO and/or the Crown

and was not under the control or supervision of the Hospital. Similarly, the oversight of his activities in the justice system rested with those who sought and retained his services.

Dr. Smith's protracted history of incorrect autopsy interpretations — presented under oath in a court of law — created a trail of victims, the falsely accused, the falsely convicted, and the falsely imprisoned. It is a path strewn with heartbreak, destroyed marriages and families, lost jobs, ruined reputations — destroyed lives — a sequence of irreparable damage that no amount of compensation could rectify.

In 1980–1981, during the apparent rise in the number of HSC cardiac ward deaths, all of these deaths had been studied carefully and discussed by the nursing staff and the attending physicians, who attributed them to natural causes.

However, based on interpretations of specimens taken in the autopsy rooms by the pathology department, these "natural deaths" suddenly became the focus of an intensive murder investigation — murder by intentional digoxin, perpetrated by the attending nursing staff.

Is it thus just a coincidence that, shortly after Dr. Smith was hired by the HSC as an anatomic pathologist, a murder theory arose, based on interpretations of specimens taken in the autopsy rooms by a pathologist? Throughout 1984, he was a member of the HSC Mortality Review Committee — the time during which Grange was writing his Inquiry Report, which appeared on December 28, 1984.

As noted earlier, the "Terms of Reference" for the Grange Inquiry prohibited assigning guilt, or the naming, or even the suggesting, of anyone he might consider responsible. It was to be solely an inquiry — a fact-finding exercise. Grange balked at the restrictions, knowingly making statements that "might well be deemed at least a partial identification of the killer or killers."

On page 4 of his Report, Grange admitted that: "Perhaps there will be some evidence which has influenced me in reaching my conclusions upon which I can neither report nor comment." This indicates that "the evidence" was not hard evidence at all, but likely represented hearsay from someone with strong persuasive powers.

Dr. Smith was on the HSC Mortality Review committee throughout the time Grange was preparing his report, released December 28, 1984. The so-called digoxin deaths would have been discussed repeatedly, and Grange would have been made aware of the contents of the discussions.

When faced with false charges of the murder of children, Susan Nelles was too strong of character to let herself become a helpless victim to the vultures of circumstance that hovered and circled around her, waiting for her to fail and fall. She adamantly refused to fall prey to and be consumed by false accusations. Instead, it was she who prevailed in the end.

Conclusion

A Role Model for Nurses Receives an Honorary Degree

There are many different wars and many different battlefields in life where valour is displayed in our history books. This particular war was waged, not against a nation, not against an army, not even against a city, but against a young nurse who, while skillfully performing her duties with care and compassion, ended up having to defend, not only herself and the honour of her family, but the integrity of the very profession she represented, standing steadfastly and almost alone, while facing assaults on many fronts. Throughout, she held her head high, displaying courage and unwavering will. In a classic battle of David versus Goliath proportions, she made Canadian legal history by successfully suing the Ontario Attorney General and the Crown Attorney for malicious prosecution.

Despite the smoke of suspicion swirling around her after Justice Samuel Grange's comments about "the murderer" and "the killer" in his report and, unfortunately, still perpetuated in some blogs by misdirected members of the legal profession, Susan Nelles steeled herself, displaying dignity and a courage that had been tested by many months of grilling in the hearings and then at the Grange Inquiry.

Derailed from her chosen field of pediatric cardiac nursing, but undaunted in the pursuit of her career, she continued to serve her chosen profession with great skill at the Toronto Hospital for Sick Children in the Dialysis Unit, until she moved to Belleville, where she became the Director of the Belleville Dialysis Unit at the Kingston General Hospital, while lecturing frequently on the legal aspects of the nursing profession in which she had risen to become an outstanding role model.

In 1999, Queen's University bestowed on Susan Nelles Pine an honourary degree at the Convocations of the School of Graduate Studies, Faculty of Health Sciences and Faculty of Law, in recognition of her courageous actions, persevering in the face of enormous adversity, citing that: "she permanently heightened nurses' awareness of the absolute necessity of protecting their integrity as professionals in the healthcare sector."

Postscript

The Irony

In 1981, the major Japanese syringe manufacturer, Terumo, felt profound shame to learn that Australian researchers, Petersen et al., had found that the natural rubber plunger seals of their disposable syringes could contaminate the syringe contents with MBT. Immediately and courageously, Terumo alerted the medical profession of this unsuspected contamination problem through the *Australia and New Zealand Journal of Medicine*. Terumo simultaneously demanded that their suppliers of pharmaceutical rubber increase immediately the quality control at the factory level to reduce the risk of MBT contamination of injections, while they developed a suitable MBT-free synthetic rubber (silicone rubber) for their syringes.

Because of Terumo's upright behaviour and their use of non-MBT silicone rubber, I used Terumo syringes exclusively in my practice when they became available in Canada. Terumo's ethical actions resulted in Japan becoming free from natural rubber in syringes and ampoule seals. Their childhood immunization vaccine unit dose syringes fell into this category.

In 2009–2010, there was a mass immunization project to protect Canadian citizens from a potentially pandemic form of influenza (H1N1). In November 2010, I read a newspaper article describing that GSK's H1N1 vaccine, Arepanrix, lot 7A, was being withdrawn from the Canadian market because of many severe allergic reactions.

The B.C. Centre for Disease Control released a chart, updated August 2010, of 28 immunization vaccines that were in contact with natural rubber. GSK manufactured six of these, including a seasonal influenza vaccine, Fluarix.

Since then, I have been badgering Health Canada to test GSK's Fluarix, lot 7A, for natural rubber contact and for MBT contamination. (To the time of writing this postscript, they have not done so, or informed me that they have — or the results if they have).

This discovery compelled me to submit an article to the *Canadian Medical Association Journal* in January 2011.

Most of the doctors, dentists, and nurses reading this book are learning about the significance of MBT contamination for the first time and must realize that MBT has been a worldwide hazard for many years. However, the MBT problem has been kept from them because medical journals choose not to print pertinent articles on the subject. My article represented the essence of what a medical journal is all about.

The article below, submitted to the *CMAJ* in the category of a Commentary article of 1,000 words, shows its final form — after a prolonged back-and-forth editing process.

MBT-latex-rubber Anaphylaxis: An Ongoing Saga

From 1860, physicians used calibrated glass syringe-needle combinations for injections.

By 1960, disposable plastic syringes achieved cleanliness, but other lingering hazards emerged.

A new rapid injection technique showing a dense vascular nephrogram phase of excretory urography (Hamilton, *CMAJ*, 1971), led to my performing 1,000 IVPs yearly. Observing patients for three minutes after injecting, while monitoring the pulse, inculcated keen awareness of adverse reactions.

In 1983, a cluster of reactions (hives) culminated in a patient with anaphylaxis. Intensive investigation revealed an allergenic toxin, mercaptobenzothiazole (MBT), leached from rubber plunger seals of plastic syringes, contaminated the dye. Thereafter, I used all-plastic, rubber-free Danish syringes.

MBT, a vulcanization catalyst, is essential to convert amorphous, doughy, raw latex into tough, resilient, natural rubber.

Unconscionably, although Health Canada proved MBT from syringes contaminated the injections, they informed me that a "phenolic compound" (a broad generic term) was the contaminant,[1] while simultaneously (May 1983) informing the manufacturers and U.S. Food and Drug Administration it was MBT. The FDA (May 1983) warned manufacturers (not physicians) that if syringes leached MBT, to consider replacing the MBT-latex-rubber seals, as one manufacturer already had.

The true nature of MBT contamination emerged when *Radiology*'s editor, Harry Fischer, cross-examined Health Canada's laboratory staff. *Radiology* (Hamilton, 1984) published the defining MBT contamination article 15 months after the manufacturers were notified.

Naturally, physicians, oblivious to the MBT-latex-rubber factor, attributed worldwide anaphylactic reactions, including deaths, to the injected pharmaceutical.

While using MBT-free syringes, another cluster of reactions arose (1986). This time, ampoule seals contaminated the injections with MBT.[2] Similar MBT-latex-rubber parts of syringes, ampoules, and IV apparatus caused reactions worldwide — invariably attributed to the injected pharmaceuticals (dental anesthetics, X-ray dyes, vaccines).

In 1981–83, 50 percent of syringe rubber leached MBT, which was falsely identified as digoxin

A surge in baby cardiac deaths (1980–1981) at the Toronto Hospital for Sick Children (HSC) was linked to intentional digoxin poisoning by nursing staff. All babies had been classified as seriously ill from admission time. Originally, attending doctors attributed all the deaths to natural causes, until interpretations of specimens taken by HSC pathologists at the autopsy tables introduced the theory of child murders.

In December 1987, Health Canada's Dr. Ed Napke suggested to me a link between the Toronto baby deaths and MBT-contaminated injections. This comment triggered the complex investigation that I continue to pursue.

Defining evidence in the *Canadian Nurse Journal* ("The Nurses are Innocent," Hamilton, 1993) proved there was no digoxin poisoning.

The most seriously ill received multiple injections, with repeated exposure to the cumulative toxin, MBT, which was being falsely measured as digoxin by the Centre of Forensic Sciences' HPLC test method, praised for its accuracy during the Grange Inquiry.

Simultaneously (1980–83), at Hammersmith Hospital, London, England, neonatal babies being monitored for theophylline levels by electrophoresis, unexpectedly demonstrated "potentially toxic" levels of MBT compounds. MBT leached from the MBT-latex-rubber of syringes, ampoule seals and IV apparatus. Each injection exposure added cumulatively to the MBT blood levels.[3] Similar unsuspected exposure to MBT occurred in hospitalized babies in Toronto and worldwide, risking death from anaphylaxis, or cumulative toxicity.

Coincidentally, disgraced pathologist Dr. Charles Smith passed the Fellowship examinations in pathology in 1980. With an avid interest in doing autopsies on children who died suddenly, he was hired by the HSC, just as the child murder theory began.

There was no digoxin poisoning and thus, no murders. "The Nurses are Innocent."

Health Canada (1989) warned that leaching of MBT into injections was "unacceptable." Potentially MBT-laden syringes were used worldwide, though less frequently in Canada.

MBT-latex-rubber was found contaminating 28 local anesthetics (1990). [4] Following a near-death experience during dental surgery, Alberta's NDP leader,

Pam Barrett, left politics. Her anaphylactic reaction was attributed to allergy to the local anesthetic. Also, in 1990, Dr. Ed Napke warned *CMAJ* readers that allergy to MBT, leached from pharmaceutical rubber, could cause "respiratory or cardiac arrest."

The FDA's 1996 "Final Rule" on pharmaceutical and medical device MBT-latex-rubber was created "in response to numerous reports of severe allergic reactions and deaths related to a wide range of medical devices containing natural rubber." It was blatantly ignored, using unenforceable terms like "recommended" and "suggested." With such phraseology, the "Final Rule" was destined to be broken. "Numerous reports of severe allergic reactions and deaths" demanded an enforced law!

In 2005, 20 percent of pharmaceutical ampoules were sealed with MBT-latex-rubber, sometimes unacknowledged in packaging or even by the manufacturer.[5]

MBT-latex-rubber in mass-produced Indian and Chinese disposable syringes exposes over half the world to MBT-contaminated injections.

GlaxoSmithKline withdrew H1N1 vaccine, lot 7A, which caused serious reactions with anaphylaxis in Manitoba (2010). This is suggestive of MBT-contaminated vaccine. CDC documents (2009) showed GSK among manufacturers of 28 vaccines in contact with MBT-latex-rubber.

Will this thirty-year saga ever end?

(Note: References below accompany the above article)

[1] Gavin Hamilton, "Adverse Reactions to Intravenous Pyelography Contrast Agents." *Canadian Medical Association Journal* (1983), Volume 129, 406–7.

[2] Gavin Hamilton, "Contamination of Contrast Agent by MBT in Rubber Seals," *Canadian Medical Association Journal*, 1987, Volume 136, 1020–21.

[3] J.H. Meek, B.R. Pettit, "Avoidable Accumulation of Potentially Toxic Levels of Benzothiazoles in Babies Intravenous Therapy." *Lancet* (1985), Volume 2, 1090–1092.

[4] C.B. Airaudo, A. Gayte-Sorbier, R. Mombura, P. Laurent, "Leaching of Antioxidants and Vulcanization Accelerators from Rubber Closures into Drug Preparations." *Journal of Biomaterials Science*, 1990, Volume 1, 231–241.

[5] R.G. Hamilton, R.H. Brown et al, "Administering Pharmaceuticals to Latex-allergic Patients from Vials Containing Natural Rubber Latex Closures." *American Journal of Health-System Pharmacy*, 2005, Volume 62, 1822–1827

Within a few days of receiving notice of the rejection of this *CMAJ* article in mid-March, 2011, I stumbled upon a pertinent news item from Japan.

Although Terumo pioneered the use of non-MBT sealing materials, by an ironic and tragic twist of fate, five Japanese babies receiving routine preventative immunization with whooping cough (pertussis) vaccine ActHIB, died of anaphylaxis in 2010 to 2011. In March 2011, the manufacturer, Sanofi Pasteur, withdrew 200,000 doses of ActHIB pediatric whooping cough vaccine. Unbeknownst to Japanese physicians, the diluent for the vaccine was listed in a U.S. CDC (Centers for Disease Control) document, August 2010, as being sealed with MBT-latex rubber (natural rubber), just as it is in North America, along with several other routine childhood immunization vaccines.

ActHIB was the first foreign-made vaccine to be imported into Japan.

———

My 1990 letter to the editor, published in the *Lancet,* finished with a request, which is even more appropriate now, 21 years later, to "ask government regulatory bodies and manufacturers when natural rubber manufactured with MBT was last used in unit dose syringes and what are the expiry dates of the drugs involved."

Appendix: Curriculum Vitae

Gavin Hamilton

— Entered the University of Western Ontario in 1949 with the
  UWO Board of Governors Prize in Physics and Chemistry
  and a scholarship in Sciences, Mathematics, and Languages,
  graduating in Medicine in 1955.
— Internal medicine residency program, July 1, 1955, to June
  30, 1957.
— Family practice, solo, in a private office, London, Ontario,
  July 1957 to June 1966.
— Diagnostic radiology residency program, Victoria Hospital,
  London, Ontario, July 1966 to June 1969.
— Fellow of the Royal College of Physicians and Surgeons of
  Canada (Diagnostic Radiology), November 1969.
— Diagnostic Radiologist, Westminster Hospital, D.V.A.,
  1970–1973.
— Private diagnostic radiology practice, Colborne-Central
  X-ray, London, mostly solo practice, with a rank of Assistant

Professor (UWO), 1973 to 1994.

— *Locum tenens* diagnostic radiology, 1994–1999.

— Retired from diagnostic radiology in 1999, while holding the rank of Assistant Professor of Diagnostic Radiology until 2001.

Articles

1. G. Hamilton, "Unilateral Decrease in Renal Vascularity on the Excretory Urogram." *Canadian Medical Association Journal*, 1971, Volume 105, 1151–54.

2. G. Hamilton, "The Vascular Nephrogram Phase of Excretory Urography and its Implications." *Radiology*, 1972, Volume 102, 37–40.

3. M.K. Hanna MK, G. Hamilton, J.K. Wyatt, "Post Prostatectomy Urinary Tract Infection." *Urology*, 1977, Volume 10, 71–78.

4. G. Hamilton, "Adverse Reactions to Intravenous Contrast Agents." *Canadian Medical Association Journal*, 1983, Volume 129, 405–06.

5. G. Hamilton, "Contamination of Contrast Agents by Rubber Components of 50 mL Disposable Plastic Syringes." *Radiology*, 1984, Volume 152, 539–40.

6. G. Hamilton, "Severe Adverse Reactions to Urography in Patients Taking Beta Adrenergic Blocking Agents." *Canadian Medical Association Journal*, 1985, Volume 133, 122.

7. G. Hamilton, "Hypotension During Urography in Patients Taking Beta-blockers." *Canadian Medical Association Journal*, 1985, Volume 30, 1201–02.

8. G. Hamilton, "Contamination of Contrast Agent by MBT in Rubber Seals." *Canadian Medical Association Journal*, 1987, Volume 136, 1020–21.

9. G. Hamilton, "Zero-added-dose Gastrointestinal Film

Studies." *Canadian Association of Radiologists Journal,* 1989, Volume 40, 203–05.

10. G. Hamilton, "Zero-added-dose Gastrointestinal Film Studies — An Update." *Canadian Association of Radiologists Journal,* 1990.

11. G. Hamilton, "Medical Rubber Anaphylaxis." *Lancet.* 1990, Volume 336, 187.

12. G. Hamilton, "A Simple Method of Producing Diagnostic Copies from Overexposed Radiographs." *Canadian Association of Radiologists Journal,* 1991, Volume 42, 216–17.

13. G. Hamilton, "The Nurses are Innocent." *Canadian Nurse Journal,* December 1993, 27–31.

14. G. Hamilton, "It's Time for Justice for the Sick Kids Nurses." *The Lawyers Weekly,* November 18, 1994.

15. G. Hamilton, "Controversy Over Ionic and Nonionic Radiopaque Contrast Media." *Canadian Association of Radiologists Journal,* 1994, Volume 45, 331.

16. G. Hamilton, "Echogenic Blood During Slow Flow," (Letter) *CARJ,* 1994, Volume 45, 487.

17. G. Hamilton, "Ultrasound Images on Thermal Paper are Best Displayed on a View Box." *CARJ,* 1997, Volume 48, 359.

Books

1. *Patterns in Fluid Flow Paradoxes: Variations on a Theme.* UWO Graphic Services, 1980.

2. *Patterns in Fluid Flow Paradoxes: Transition to Turbulence.* UWO Graphic Services, 2005

3. *Coherent Sound Energy in Transition to Turbulence.* UWO Graphic Services, 2008

4. *Transition to Turbulence — Dynamic Standing Waves* ©, Internet posting, 2009

5. *Order in Chaos — The Physics of Transition to Turbulence,*
    Aylmer Express, Aylmer, Ontario, July 2011.

Notes

Chapter One

1. William Harvey, *Exercitatio Anatomica de Motu Cordis et Sanguinis in Animalibus* (1628).
2. Gavin Hamilton, "The Vascular Nephrogram Phase of Excretory Urography and its Implications," *Radiology*, 1972, Volume 102, 37–40.
3. Gavin Hamilton, "Unilateral Decrease in Renal Vascularity on the Excretory Urogram," *Canadian Medical Association Journal*, 1971, Volume 105, 1151–54.
4. Gavin Hamilton, "The Vascular Nephrogram Phase of Excretory Urography and its Implications," *Radiology*, 1972, Volume 102, 37–40.

Chapter Two

1. K. Brockow, C. Christiansen, G. Kanny, et al., "Management of Hypersensitivity Reactions to Iodinated Contrast Media," *Allergy*, 2005, Volume 60, Issue 2, 150–58.
2. Gavin Hamilton, "Severe Adverse Reactions to Urography in Patients Taking Beta-Adrenergic Blocking Agents," *Canadian Medical Association Journal*, 1985, Volume 133, 122.
3. Gavin Hamilton, "Hypotension During Urography in Patients Taking Beta-Blockers," *Canadian Medical Association Journal*, 1985, Volume 133, 1201–02.

Chapter Four

1. Gavin Hamilton, "Adverse Reactions to Intravenous Pyelography Contrast Agents," *Canadian Medical Association Journal*, 1983, Volume 129, 405–06.
2. J.R. Thornbury, H.C. Redman, "In Memoriam: Harry Fischer," *Radiology*, 1999, Volume 212, 913–14.

Chapter Five

1. Gavin Hamilton, "Contamination of Contrast Agents by Rubber Components of 50 mL Disposable Plastic Syringes," *Radiology*, 1984, Volume 152, 539–40.
2. *Ibid.*
3. M.C. Petersen, J.H. Vine, J.J. Ashley, and R.L. Nation, "Leaching a Contaminant into the Contents of Disposable Syringes," *Australia and New Zealand Medical Journal*, 1981, Volume 11, 208–09.
4. M.C. Petersen, et al., "Leaching of H-MBT into the Contents of Disposable Plastic Syringes," *Journal of Pharmaceutical*

Sciences, 1981, Volume 70, 1139–42.

5. Terumo (Australia PTY Ltd), "Leaching of a Contaminant into the Contents of Disposable Syringes," *Australia and New Zealand Journal of Medicine*, 1981, Volume 11, 435.

6. Harry M. Meyer, Jr., MD, director, National Center for Drugs and Biologics, Department of Health and Human Services, "Letter to all Registrants (Medical Rubber, Syringe, and Drug manufacturers)," May 23, 1983.

7. J.J. Reepmeyer, Y.H. Juhl, "Contamination of Injectable Solutions with 2-mercaptobenzothiazole Leached from Rubber Closures," *The Journal of Pharmaceutical Sciences*, 1983, Volume 72, 1302–05.

8. C.L. Dubin, J. Gilchrist, H. McDonald, H. Nadler, M.R. Guberman, J. Auksi, "Report of the Hospital for Sick Children Review Committee," January 1983, 205–07.

Chapter Six

1. W.L. Guess, R.K. O'Leary, "Toxicity of a Rubber Accelerator," *Toxicology and Applied Pharmacology*, 1969, Volume 14, 221-31.

2. M.C. Petersen, J. Vine, J.J. Ashley, R.L. Nation, "Leaching of 2-(2-hydroxyethylmercapto) Benzothiazole into Contents of Disposable Syringes," *Journal of Pharmaceutical Sciences*, 1981, Volume 70, 1139–43.

3. Gavin Hamilton, "Adverse Reactions to Intravenous Pyelography Contrast Agents," 406–07.

4. Gavin Hamilton, "Contamination of Contrast Agents by Rubber Components of 50 mL Disposable Plastic Syringes," *Radiology*, 1984, Volume 152, 539–40.

5. G. Salmona, A. Assaf, Gayte-Sorbier, C.B. Airaudo, "Mass Spectral Identification of Benzothiazole Derivatives Leached into Injections by Disposable Syringes," *Biomedical Mass Spectrometry*, 1984, Volume 11, 450–52.

6. A. Korhonen, K. Hemminki, K. Vainio, "Embryotoxicity of Benzothiazoles, Benzenesulfohydrazide, and Dithiodimorpholine to the Chicken Embryo," *Archives of Environmental Contamination and Toxicology,* 1982, Volume 11, 753–59.

7. F.M. Keim, "The Impact of Medical Devices on Quality Control of Pharmaceuticals," *The Journal of the Parenteral Drug Association,* 1978, Volume 32, 33–38.

8. Reepmeyer, Juhl, 1302–05.

9. *Ibid.*

10. Guess, O'Leary, 221–31.

11. Reepmeyer, Juhl, 1302–05.

Chapter Seven

1. Health and Welfare Canada, Health Protection Branch, Notes Number 11, "Leachates in Injectable Drugs." April 1989.

2. Gavin Hamilton, "Medical Rubber Anaphylaxis." *Lancet,* 1990, Volume 336, 187.

3. J. Weissinger, Assistant Director (Pharmacology/Toxicology), Office of Drug Evaluation II, FDA, Rockville, Maryland, U.S., personal letter, May 1, 1990.

4. R.G. Hamilton, R.H. Brown, et al, "Administering Pharmaceuticals to Latex-allergic Patients from Vials Containing Natural Rubber Latex Closures." *American Journal of Health-System Pharmacy Society,* 2005, Volume 62, 1822–27.

5. Reepmeyer, Juhl, 1302–05.

6. D.W. Gelfand, "Barium Enemas, Latex Balloons, and Anaphylactic Reactions." *American Journal of Roentgenology,*. 1991, Volume 156 (1), 1–2.

7. E-Z-EM Inc., Division of Therapex, Anjou, Quebec, Urgent Medical Alert, October 9, 1990.

8. L.E. Gaul, "Results of Patch Testing with Rubber Antioxidants and Accelerators." *Journal of Investigative Dermatology*, 1957, Volume 29, 105–10.

9. Reepmeyer, Juhl, 1302–05.

10. Guess, O'Leary, 221–31.

11. Y. Hirai, Y. Sanada, T. Fujiwara, S. Hasegawa, N. Kuwabara, "High calorie Infusion-induced Hepatic Impairments in Infants," *Journal of Parenteral Nutrition*, 1979, Volume 3, 146–50.

12. Gavin Hamilton, "Contamination of Contrast Agents by Rubber Components of 50 mL Disposable Plastic Syringes," 539–40.

13. R.G. Hamilton, R.H. Brown, et al., "Administering Pharmaceuticals to Latex-allergic Patients from Vials Containing Natural Rubber Latex Closures," *American Journal of Health-System Pharmacy Society Journal of Health-System Pharmacy Society*, 2005, Volume 62, 1822–27.

14. Guess, O'Leary, 221–31.

15. J.H. Meek, Pettit, B.R., "Avoidable Accumulation of Potentially Toxic Levels of Benzothiazoles in Babies Receiving Intravenous Therapy," *Lancet*, 1985, Volume 2, 1090–92.

Chapter Eight

1. M. Angell, "Excess in the Pharmaceutical Industry," *New England Journal of Medicine*, 2004, Volume 171, 1451–53.

2. L.K. Altman, "New England Journal of Medicine Names Third Editor in a Year," *New York Times*, May 21, 2000.

3. John Hoey, "Editorial Independence and the Canadian Medical Association Journal," *New England Journal of Medicine*, 2006, Volume 354, 1982–83.

4. J.P. Kassirer, F. Davidoff, K. O'Hara, D.A. Redelmeier, "Editorial Autonomy of the *CMAJ*," *Canadian Medical Association Journal*, 2006, Volume 174, 945–50.

5. G. Harris, "Caustic Government Report Deals Blow to Diabetes Drug," *New York Times,* July 10, 2010.

6. G. Harris, "Drug Maker Hid Test Data, Files Indicate," *New York Times*, July 13, 2010.

7. *Ibid.*

8. Steven E. Nissen, Kathy Wolski, "Effect of Rosiglitazone on the Risk of Myocardial Infarction and Death from Cardiovascular Causes," *New England Journal of Medicine,* 2007, Volume 356, 2457–71.

9. R. Smith, "Medical Journals and Pharmaceutical Companies: Uneasy Bedfellows," *British Medical Journal,* 2003, Volume 326, 1202–05.

10. J. Lexchin J, D.W. Light, "Commercial Influence and the Content in Medical Journals," *British Medical Journal,* 2006, Volume 332, 1444–47.

11. MS. Wilkes, B.H. Doblin, M.F. Shapiro, "Pharmaceutical Advertisements in Leading Medical Journals," *Annals of Internal Medicine,* 1992, Volume 116, 912–19.

12. *Ibid.*

13. Editorial, "Our Conflicted Medical Journals," *New York Times,* 2006, June 23, 2006.

14. Medical Research Council of Canada, Natural Sciences and Engineering Research Council of Canada, Social Sciences and Humanities Research Council of Canada. Tri-Council Policy Statement: Ethical Conduct for Research Involving Humans, Ottawa: The Councils, 1998.

15. N.F. Olivieri, G.M. Brittenham, C.E. McLaren, D.M. Templeton, R.A. McClelland et al, "Long-term Safety and Effectiveness of Iron-chelation Therapy with Deferiprone for Thalassemia Major," *New England Journal of Medicine,* 1998, Volume 339, 417–23.

16. E. Gibson, F. Baylis, S. Lewis, "Dances With the Pharmaceutical Industry," *Canadian Medical Association Journal,* 2002, Volume 166, 448–50.

17. J. Thompson, P. Baird, J. Downie. "Report of the Commission of Inquiry on the Case Involving Dr. Nancy Olivieri, the Hospital for Sick Children, the University of Toronto, and Apotex Inc.," (Toronto: Canadian Association of University Teachers), 2000, 100.

18. Cicero, *De Legibus*, 51 B.C.E *"Salus populi suprema lex esto."* (The health and welfare of the people reign supreme.)

19. The University of Winnipeg: Awards and Distinctions, Honorary Doctor of Science, Autumn, 2006.

20. E. Gibson, F. Baylis, S. Lewis, 448–50.

21. J. Magder, "McGill Professor Caught in Ghostwriting Scandal." *Montreal Gazette*, August 24, 2009.

22. A. Naimark, B.M Knoppers, F.H. Lowy, "Clinical Trials of L1 (deferiprone) at the Hospital for Sick Children: a Review of Facts and Circumstances. Part IV: Issues and Findings," (Toronto: The Hospital for Sick Children, 2000).

23. J. Thompson, P. Baird, J. Downie, 100.

24. *Ibid,* 448.

Chapter Nine

1. J.J. Caro, E. Trindade, M. McGregor, "The Risks of Death and of Severe Nonfatal Reactions With High-vs-Low-Osmolality Contrast Media: a Meta-Analysis," *American Journal of Roentgenology*, 1991, Volume 156, 825–32.

2. H. Katayama H, K. Yamaguchi, T. Kozuka, et al, "Adverse Reactions to Ionic and Nonionic Contrast Media. A Report from the Japanese Committee on the Safety of Contrast Media," *Radiology,* Volume 175, 621–28.

3. D.J. Roy, T. Dickens, M. McGregor, "The Choice of Contrast Media: Medical, Ethical and Legal Considerations," *Canadian Medical Association Journal*, 1992, Volume 147, 1321–24.

4. Gavin Hamilton, "Controversy Over Ionic and Nonionic Radiopaque Contrast Media," *Canadian Association of Radiologists Journal,* 1994, Volume 4, 331.

5. H. Katayama H, K. Yamaguchi, T. Kozuka, et al, "Adverse Reactions to Ionic and Nonionic Contrast Media. A Report from the Japanese Committee on the Safety of Contrast Media," *Radiology,* Volume 175, 621–28.

6. Gavin Hamilton, "Contamination of Contrast Agent by MBT in Rubber Seals," *Canadian Medical Association Journal,* 1987, Volume 136, 1020–21.

7. C.S. Houston, personal letter, December 6, 1994, paraphrasing Isaiah 40: 3.

8. E.C. Lasser, G.L. Lyon, C.C Berry, "Reports on Contrast Media Reactions: Analysis of Data from Reports to the U.S. Food and Drug Administration," *Radiology,* 1997, Volume 203, 605–10.

Chapter Ten

1. E. Napke, "Out of the Closet." Book review (*Formulation Factors in Adverse Reactions,* A.T. Florence, 1990), *Canadian Medical Association Journal,* 1990, Volume 143, 1036–37.

2. Gavin Hamilton, "Medical Rubber Anaphylaxis," *Lancet,* 1990, Volume 336, 187.

3. FDA, Guidance for Industry User Labeling for Devices that Contain Natural Rubber (CFR 801.437); Small Entity Compliance Guide for Industry, document issued on: April 1, 2003, U.S. Department of Health and Human Services, Food and Drug Administration, Center for Devices and Radiological Health, Office of Compliance.

4. Institute on Disability and Human Development (IDHD)/ DHD, University of Illinois: Alert! Newsletter. Mandatory labelling: (Sept. 30, 1998), Spring 2005, Volume 11, No. 2.

5. R.G. Hamilton, R.H. Brown, et al, "Administering Pharmaceuticals to Latex-allergic Patients from Vials Containing Natural Rubber Latex Closures," *American Journal of Health-System Pharmacy*, 2005, Volume 62, 1822–27.

6. FDA, Health and Human Services: Natural rubber-containing devices; user labeling. Final Rule, (1998); August 31; 63 (168), 46174–75.

7. R.P. Hoffman, "Latex Hypersensitivity in a Child with Diabetes," *Archives of Pediatric and Adolescent Medicine*, 2000, 281–82.

8. J. Mahoney, "Alberta NDP Leader Quits After Near-death Experience," *Globe and Mail* (February 2, 2000).

9. C.B. Airaudo, A. Gayte-Sorbier, R. Mombura, P. Laurent, "Leaching of Antioxidants and Vulcanization Accelerators from Rubber Closures into Drug Preparations," *Journal of Biomaterials Science*, 1990, Volume 1, 231–41.

10. M.T. Cicero, *De Legibus*, 51 B.C.E.

11. FDA, Health and Human Services: Natural rubber-containing devices; user labeling. Final Rule, (1998); August 31; 63 (168), 46174–75.

12. Gavin Hamilton, "Medical Rubber Anaphylaxis," *Lancet*, 187.

13. The Honourable Allan Rock, personal letter, January 23, 2001.

14. M.J. Primeau, "Natural Rubber Pharmaceutical Vial Closures Release Latex Allergens that Produce Skin Reactions," *Allergy and Clinical Immunology*, 2001, Volume 107, 958–62.

15. A.R. Shojae, D.A. Haas, "Local Anesthetic Cartridges and Latex Allergy: a Literature Review," *Journal of the Canadian Dental Association*, 2002, Volume 68, 622–26.

16. Gavin Hamilton, "Medical Rubber Anaphylaxis," *Lancet*, 14

17. Gavin Hamilton, "Contamination of Contrast Agents by Rubber Components of 50 mL Disposable Plastic Syringes," 539–540.

18. Gavin Hamilton, "Contamination of Contrast Agent by MBT in Rubber Seals," 1020–21.

19. C.B. Airaudo, A. Gayte-Sorbier, R. Mombura, P. Laurent, "Leaching of Antioxidants and Vulcanization Accelerators from Rubber Closures into Drug Preparations," 231–41.

20. FDA, Health and Human Services: Natural rubber-containing devices; user labelling: Final rule; (1998); August 31; 63 (168); 46174–75.

21. R.G. Hamilton, R.H. Brown, et al., 1822–27.

22. C.B. Airaudo, et al., 231–41.

23. Kinsella and MacLeod, "Deaths at Sick Kids May Not Be Murder," *The Ottawa Citizen*, February 23, 1989.

Chapter Eleven

1. E. Napke, "Out of the Closet," 1036–37.

2. Gavin Hamilton, "Severe Adverse Reactions to Urography in Patients Taking Beta-Adrenergic Blocking Agents," *Canadian Medical Association Journal*, 1985, Volume 133, 122.

3. Gavin Hamilton, "Hypotension During Urography in Patients Taking Beta-Blockers." *Canadian Medical Association Journal*, 1985, Volume 133, 1201–02.

4. J.H. Toogood, "Beta-blocker Therapy and the Risk of Anaphylaxis." *Canadian Medical Association Journal*, 1987, Volume 136, 929–33.

5. D.M. Lang, M.B. Alpern, P.F. Vistainer, S.T. Smith, "Increased Risk for Anaphylactoid Reaction from Contrast Media in Patients on β-adrenergic Blockers with Asthma," *Annals of Internal Medicine*, 1991, Volume 115, 270–76.

6. S.K. Morcos, "Acute Serious and Fatal Reactions to Contrast Media: Our Current Understanding," *The British Journal of Radiology*, 2005, Volume 78, 686–93.

7. H.S. Thomsen, *Contrast Media: Safety Issues and ESUR Guidelines* (Berlin/Heidelberg: Springer, 2006), Chapter 4.2 (Risk Factors), 19–20.

8. Guess, O'Leary, 221–31.
9. Reepmeyer, Juhl, 1302–05.

Chapter Thirteen

1. Samuel Grange, P.S.A. Lamek, E.A. Cronk, T. Millar, Royal Commission of Inquiry into Certain deaths at the Hospital for Sick Children and Related Matters, December 28, 1984.
2. Austin Cooper, "The Defence of Innocence," in *Counsel for the Defence: The Bernard Cohen Memorial Lectures in Criminal Law*, edited by E.I. Greenspan (Toronto: Irwin Law, 2005).
3. D.A. Harris, "Decision in Nelles Case a Defining Moment," *Burlington Post*, March 7, 2001.

Chapter Fourteen

1. Guess, O'Leary, 221–31.

Chapter Fifteen

1. C.L. Dubin, J. Gilchrist, H. McDonald, H. Nadler, F.M.R. Guberman, J. Auski, Report of the Hospital for Sick Children Review Committee (January 1983).
2. Ted Bissland, *Death Shift: The Digoxin Murders at Sick Kids* (Toronto: Methuen, 1988).

Chapter Seventeen

1. Bissland, 53.
2. Grange et al., 21.

3. Grange et al., 30
4. Peter Macklem, personal communication, April 2, 2010.
5. Bissland, 35.
6. Gavin Hamilton, "It's Time for Justice for the Sick Kids Nurses," *The Lawyers Weekly,* November 18, 1994.

Chapter Eighteen

1. Grange et al., 23.
2. *Ibid.,* 21.
3. *Ibid.*
4. Kinsella and MacLeod, "Deaths at Sick Kids May Not Be Murder," *The Ottawa Citizen*, February 23, 1989
5. Gavin Hamilton, "It's Time for Justice for the Sick Kids Nurses."
6. D.W. Seccombe, M.R. Pudek, K.H. Humphries, "Minimizing Analytical Interferences from Digoxin-like Immunoreactive Substances (DLIS) in Cases of Digoxin Toxicity," *Journal of Forensic Sciences,* 1987, Volume 32, 650–57.
7. Gavin Hamilton, "The Nurses are Innocent," *Canadian Nurse*, December 1993, 31.
8. *Ibid.,* 27–32.
9. Gavin Hamilton, "It's Time for Justice for the Sick Kids Nurses."
10. Bissland, 35.
11. Reepmeyer, Juhl, 1302–05.

Chapter Nineteen

1. Reepmeyer, Juhl, 1302–05.
2. Gavin Hamilton, "The Nurses are Innocent," 27–32.
3. J.H. Meek, Pettit, B.R., "Avoidable Accumulation of Potentially Toxic Levels of Benzothiazoles in Babies Receiving Intravenous Therapy," *Lancet,* 1985, Volume 2, 1090–92.

4. Guess, O'Leary, 221–31.

5. Gavin Hamilton, "The Nurses are Innocent," 27–32.

Chapter Twenty

1. R.P. Hoffman, "Latex Hypersensitivity in a Child with Diabetes," *Archives of Pediatric and Adolescent Medicine,* 2000, 281–82.

2. Guess, O'Leary, 221–31.

3. Meek, Pettit, 1090–92.

4. Y. Hirai, Y. Sanada, T. Fujiwara, S. Hasegawa, N. Kuwabara, "High Calorie Infusion-Induced Hepatic Impairments in Infants," *Journal of Parenteral Nutrition,* 1979, Volume 3, 146–50.

5. E.C. Lasser, G.L. Lyon, C.C. Berry, "Reports on Contrast Media Reactions: Analysis of Data from Reports to the U.S. Food and Drug Administration," *Radiology,* 1997, Volume 203, 605–10.

6. *Ibid,* 1143.

7. Guess, O'Leary, 221–31.

8. M.C. Petersen, J.H. Vine, J.J. Ashley, and R.L. Nation, "Leaching of a Contaminant into the Contents of Disposable Syringes," *Australia and New Zealand Medical Journal,* 1981, Volume 11, 208–09.

9. M.C. Petersen, J.H. Vine, J.J. Ashley, and R.L. Nation, "Leaching 2-(2-Hydroxyethylmercapto) Benzothiazole into Contents of Disposable Syringes," *Journal of Pharmaceutical Sciences,* 1981, Volume 70, 1139–43.

10. Meek, Pettit, 1090–92.

11. *Ibid.*

12. Guess, O'Leary, 221–31.

13. Reepmeyer, Juhl, 1302–05.

14. *Ibid.,* 1143.

15. C.B. Airaudo, Professor and Head of the Department of Pharmacy, Centre Hospitalier Specialise Valvert, Marseilles, France, Personal letter #002436, September 15, 1992.
16. Reepmeyer, Juhl, 1302–05.

Chapter Twenty-One

1. Bissland, 53.
2. Reepmeyer, Juhl, 1302–05.

Chapter Twenty-Two

1. Kinsella and MacLeod, "Deaths at Sick Kids May Not be Murder." *The Ottawa Citizen*, February 23, 1989.

Chapter Twenty-Three

1. Gavin Hamilton, "The Nurses are Innocent," 27–32.
2. Meek, Pettit, 1090–92.
3. Gavin Hamilton, "It's Time for Justice for the Sick Kids Nurses."

Chapter Twenty-Four

1. Bissland, 53.

Chapter Twenty-Five

1. Gavin Hamilton, "The Nurses are Innocent," 31.
2. Gavin Hamilton, "It's Time for Justice for the Sick Kids Nurses."

Index